A
Islay No

by

C. Gordon Booth

Published by Islay Museums Trust
Printed by Orr, Pollock & Co. Ltd.,
2 Crawfurd Street, Greenock.

The Museum Management Committee
gratefully acknowledges the help of
the Highlands and Islands Developement Board
in the Production of this book.

ISBN 0 9509351 0 7

For
CAROL-ANN
and Ileachs of her generation.

The cover design is from the author's bookplate,
by William Littlewood, Reading.

Contents

Introduction

MUCH has been written about the early history of Islay, the carved stones and crosses have been adequately recorded, there are several studies of the place names, which are usually so descriptive, and their Gaelic and Norse origins tell much about the island although so little is known about the activities of the Vikings. The rule of the lands of the Lordship of the Isles is well chronicled, the battle of Traigh Gruinart and much more is celebrated by the bards for those who are fortunate enough to have the Gaelic, J. F. Campbell and others have recorded a great deal of folklore, there are reports on the archaeology, a subject which will be covered in detail in the forthcoming Islay volume of the Royal Commission on the Ancient and Historic Monuments of Scotland Inventory of Ancient Monuments. The geology and natural history of the island are of such interest that they have attracted many students. Recent economic and social history are the subject of Dr. Storrie's book "Islay: Biography of an Island."

A great many volumes of Tours in the Hebrides mention Islay but a lot of the authors had never set foot on the island and took their material from tourists like Martin Martin (1703) and Thomas Pennant, who was here with the botanist John Lightfoot in 1772. The Statistical Account of 1794 and the New Statistical Account of 1845 tell something about the people but little has been published about their way of life. These extracts from my note books are about the day to day life of the people who lived here.

The material in this Note Book is taken from books and papers in the Museum library; the photographs are from the collection in the Museum, and art work by Carol-Ann Smith, the keeper.

Early Days in Islay

I AM very conscious at the time of writing that an Inventory, prepared over a number of years by experts from the Royal Commission on the Ancient and Historical Monuments in Scotland, is being printed and will be published soon, and I considered whether it would be wise to write about the early history, but as my purpose is only to demonstrate, by using a selection of published material, that Islay has been occupied by a considerable number of people for a very long time, I decided to go ahead and hope that my errors were not too many and not too serious. I believe that many visitors would like to have available a short paper about the early history to enable them to derive greater enjoyment from their stay and I hope those who want to know more will be stimulated to consult the Inventory.

The pre-history of Islay is not easily understood and one must use a great deal of imagination to build up a picture from what has been learnt by investigation and excavation, bearing in mind that isolated pieces of evidence may be entirely unrepresentative of the normal life of the community.

Dr. Lamont writes that "Islay has no relics of the Paleolithic age, but traces of Mesolithic settlement, principally of 'kitchen middens' of small mobile communities, which are found in the vicinity of the 25 foot raised beaches" which were formed before 2500 BC when the sea was roughly at its present level, and says "It was, however, in the New Stone Age (2700-1300 BC) that men took effective possession, pasturing their domestic herds, practising a simple agriculture, and interring their noble dead in impressive chambered cairns. These multi-chambered tombs in Islay have in many cases been robbed of their cairns and left open to the sky." There is more evidence from the Bronze Age (1300-200 BC). Of the next period, the Early Iron Age up to 500 AD, he said we can speak with more confidence. "Coming from the continent and sweeping over Britain from east to west, then crossing the Irish Sea, a military aristocracy of Celtic origin came to dominate the land and impose its way of life on the indigenous peoples." Also "the Early Iron Age is credited, broadly speaking, with the numerous 'duns' around the coasts and the hill fortifications. These structures vary from quite small refuges to the impressive strongholds. Here again, of course dating can only be presumptive, pending systematic excavation." One must bear in mind that the transition from one style of life to the next was gradual and there was considerable overlap.

What is believed to be the head of an Irish elk, which was found in a peat bog at Kildalton in 1870, provides one of our first problems. Was this from an animal which was cut off when the ice bridge connecting Islay to Ireland melted more than 6,000 years ago? If so it is our oldest artefact. Or was it a trophy which had been brought to the island? In that case how did it get into a peat bog? More details about the circumstance of its finding, such as how deep it was in the peat, would help to solve the problem.

The caves, most of which are round the Mull of Oa and the northeast corner of the island, have been there a long time but are almost unexplored and very little is known about them. There is evidence that those at Port a' Chotain, near Bholsa, had been occupied in the 17th or early 18th century. There are remains of old buildings on a green patch on the shore below. The cave at Bholsa is the biggest in the west of Scotland. When Pennant visited it in 1772 there were three farmers living in it with their stock and crops and at times in the summer months as many as twelve families were known to stay in it at once and it was the headquarters of those employed in the manufacture of kelp. It has not been found how far it penetrates and strange folklore has grown up around it. Here is an exciting expedition for somebody and one wonders what would be revealed by an examination of midden waste.

There are many references to our caves but the writers do not seem to have gone beyond the entrances and we are left wondering what they are like inside and most importantly whether they were ever lived in, and if so, by whom. William Macdonald in "Sketches of Islay" says Sanaig cave is worthy of notice, it is difficult to enter, its numerous far winding passages form a "perfect subterranean labyrinth," and it is most remarkable for its reverberation. On the west coast of the Oa there is Slochd Mhaol-Doraidh, the Court of the Sea King. In front of the entrance there is a pillar of rock forty feet high, called the Soldier Rock, and the entrance itself is so narrow as only to admit a small boat, and then only in fine weather. The way in is

Reconstruction of a Roundhouse excavated at Ardnave.

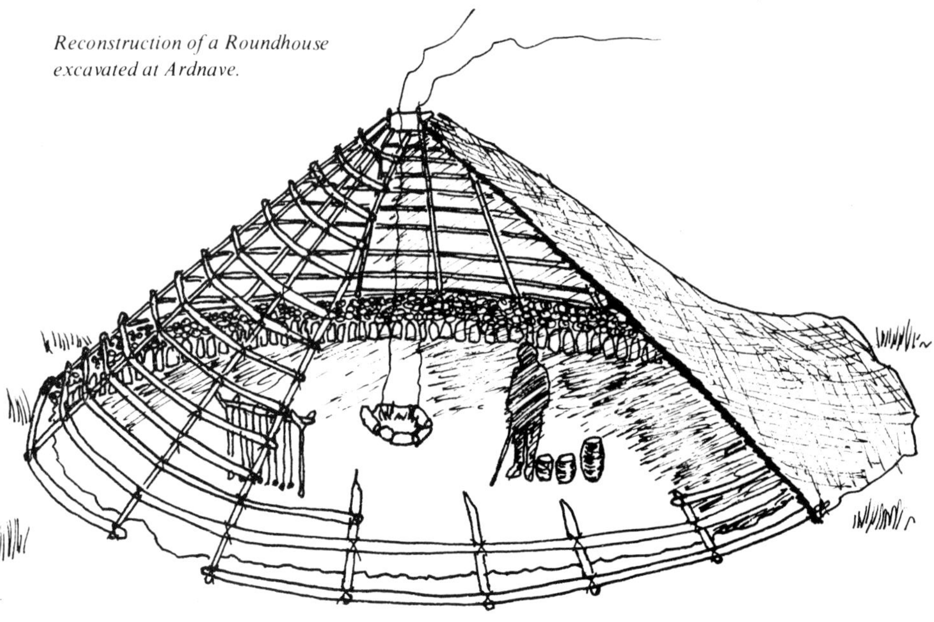

so low that one has to stoop on entering, but inside the cave there is a large water-floored hall with two recesses off. One has been explored and terminates in a small gravelly beach but the only mention of occupation is by large numbers of rock doves. At the Heights of Laggan, J. G. MacNeill tells, there are An Uamha Dhorcha, the Dark Cave; Uamha Mhic Neacail, MacNicol's Cave; and Uamah nan Calaman, the Doves' Cave. The entrance to the Dark Cave is almost invisible but the chamber inside is large. The Doves' Cave is a long cleft at the corner of Creag an Fhithich, the Raven's Rock. Of MacNicol's he says it is "a comfortable cave dwelling," but nothing further.

On the Rhinns there is Wester Ellister — West cave seat — from the Norse Hellis-setr, cave residence, and there is a cave on the shore below the farmhouse. At Cultoon there is a deep narrow dale in which there is a den that probably had been used as a human habitation.

Perhaps one of the best subjects about which to exercise one's imagination, and any detective urge one may have, is the standing stones, which are to be found all over the island singly, in groups or in one case in an ellipse. Some a few feet tall others up to 18 feet. Some may be considered in line — pointing where? One at Duisker has a flat stone slab on the ground to the north of it some yards away; standing on the slab and looking over the upright stone points to Kildalton — but is there any significance? MacNeill Weir in his "New Guide to Islay" says "There is no trace of carving on these stones and we have no clue to their significance" and I think that is still true. Dr. W. D. Lamont writes "There is a general presumption that, as the long-cairn gallery-graves were Neolithic, so the standing-stones — whether specially dressed and squared or raised in their crude state, whether single, in twos, or threes, or in circles — belong to the Bronze Age. Some of them, particularly the tall dressed stones of the Ballinaby and Kildalton districts, may in fact be much later, perhaps of the early Christian or even Viking period; but failing evidence to the contrary, a Bronze Age dating may be presumed." Diana Leatham in "Celtic Sunrise" says "In pre-Christian times upright stones, sometimes of colossal size, were used to mark graves or important places." Wilson reports in "Prehistoric Annals of Scotland" (1863) that "a large standing stone, which had long been overthrown, and lay prostrate at a little distance from Sunderland House was blasted with gunpowder and removed, in the process of levelling and draining the ground for agricultural purposes. Immediately underneath the stone lay a cist containing several rude cinerary urns, and alongside of it were found a gold fibula and an armilla of a peculiar type made from a broad band of gold beaten out so as to form a convex centre, on each side of which was a fluted ornamental border, and a raised rim returned at the edge."

The stone circle at Cultoon is the only one of this type in Islay. Professor A. Thom found that the stones could have been along the perimeter of an accurately drawn ellipse using the "Megolithic yard" (2.72 ft.). Later excavation under the direction of Dr. Euan MacKie found that the work of building the circle was never completed and owing to a miscalculation or perhaps an unfavourable omen, was abandoned. (Is it possible that for some reason, such as disease, the manpower became too weak to handle these massive stones? Was the building of the tomb known as The Giant's Grave, marked Sloch Measach on the map, just south of Beinn Tart 'a Mhill also abandoned?). It was discovered that the peat only began to grow after the site was abandoned and a radiocarbon date for the beginning of this growth gave about 1000 BC. A deposit of cremated bones, probably human, was found at a place exactly on the elliptical perimeter of the circle. To the north there is a natural mound with a small standing stone on its south side and on the top of the mound a deposit of charred branches, twigs and nuts was found under the peat and carbon dated 1300-1360 BC.

Not in any way connected but of no less interest and speculation are a few cup stones. Be alert for stones with natural pebble and water worn cups two to three inches across which could have been transported from the shore. This cannot, of course, apply to outcrop rock such as that at the old village of Tockmal on the Oa, which has a group of shallow cups. What were they used for, if at all? It has been suggested that such small cups and a pebble were an ancient form of mortar and pestle — for grinding what? One idea is that they ground fish bones for their calcium content; a reasonable enough guess, but did these people know the value of calcium?

James R. Nicolson in "Traditional Life in Shetland" says that curious cup-shaped hollows are found cut into the surface of a flat rock. They were carved laboriously out of the solid rock hundreds of years ago for the purpose of pounding soe, or ground bait, a practice that continued until late in the 19th century.

The best known of the cup-marked stones in Islay is outside the chapel at Kilchiaran; it has a couple of dozen cups, two of which pierce through the slab. It has been suggested that this stone was brought from the Cultoon circle but there is no evidence that it was ever there and no good reason has been given for making such a move.

What can we learn from twenty prehistoric burial chambers, which we call cists, and which have been uncovered up to now? If their positions are marked on a map of the island it will be seen that the main concentrations are in the Ardnave-Sanaig area, with a few down the Rhinns to Port Charlotte, another group within the sweep of Laggan Bay and a third near Kildalton. It would be unwise to come to any firm conclusion, remembering that the majority of those we know about are amongst the sandhills which are constantly being eroded by the winds which expose them, that the eastern part of the island down to Kildalton is largely deer forest which is rarely visited except by stalkers, that there are probably many more cists to be discovered, and that some have been destroyed unrecognised. However, it does seem that those on the Rhinns and the shores of Loch Indaal are near natural anchorages and fresh water and that a large section of the island was occupied by these early inhabitants.

More detailed examination shows that the burial at Cnoc na Faire, Ardnave, contained the skeleton of a girl and under her there was a rusty object which might have been a spear head. Also on Ardnave, just east of the Loch, there was a short cist with an unaccompanied cremation burial with a clay vessel and burnt bone. Not far away, on the shore of Loch Gruinart the map shows Traigh nan Cisteachan — the beach of the cists — Although none have been found here yet there are signs of an early occupation. A burial with a Bronze Age urn was found at Garreallabus halfway up the loch. At Sanaigmore a cist contained a crouched skeleton of a mature adult with knees well drawn up; and this cist was unusual in that the northern end was shaped into a point. Almost over on the west coast at Traigh Bhan there are three cists close together in the eroded sand dunes at the mouth of Glen Tuath. One contained two inhumations and a food vessel, the second fragments of inhumation, and the third had been disturbed and no remains were found.

At Ballinaby there were two Viking graves, one contained two axes, an adze, a hammer, forge tongs, an iron sword sheath, an iron boss of a shield, an iron spear and the handle of an iron pot. In the other were a pair of brooches ornamented with silver wire, silver hairpins, a plaited silver wire chain, a glass linen smoother and other relics. Two swords, a pike head and many human bones were also found. The New Statistical Account (1845) says "During the last ten years, several stone coffins were discovered in the conical hills below Sunderland farm; . . . some contained one or two urns of rudely formed unbaked clay; others contained skulls and other human bones." There is a megolithic tomb reported below Dun Chroisprig.

At Sloch Measach on the south slope of Beinn Tart A Mhill there is the structure of huge stones known as "The Giant's Grave." There could be some speculation as to whether this, like Cultoon Circle not far away, was left unfinished. Quite near, at NR215566, by the source of the Nereabolls burn one of a more normal size was found. In the field immediately south of Port Charlotte there is a four-part chambered cairn with a substantial forecourt in which recent excavation discovered neolithic pottery, two leaf arrowheads, and flint knives, and which has been dated 2650 BC. A little further south there is a cairn with a cist, below Cnoc a Chuirn, and a small cairn within an enclosing wall.

Across Loch Indaal, not far from the mouth of the Laggan river there is an important site at Cruach Mhor where pottery spanning 4,000 years indicates long occupation; some of it late Neolithic, late Bronze Age and glazed medieval. Flint arrow heads and many waste flakes have been found and there was half of a stone mace head of the period 1500-2000 BC. There have been exciting relics of probably Norse inhabitants, including fragments of brass and bronze, two jet beads and one of glass, two oval tortoise shell brooches in bronze of 9th or 10th century AD and a soapstone spindle whorl. There was also a bronze Highland brooch of 16th or 17th century origin. Further south on the Big Strand an unusual cist, divided into two storeys by a flat slab of stone, with an inhumation in the lower, found at Cnoc Aingle was considered to be early Christian, and at Kintra at the south end of the bay, blown sand revealed an extended inhumation covered by several layers of slabs, but there were no grave goods.

On the side of the road climbing up the Oa, at Cragabus, a much disturbed cist of three chambers contained unburnt human bones and a few pot sherds.

In a cist at Brahunisary in the Kildalton area there was a skeleton and a large quantity of flint flakes and chips. At Ballynaughton a Neolithic cist was later used as a depository for a coin hoard, no doubt being chosen as being safe because of the fear of the islanders about the consequences of the desecration of a burial place.

At Keills a stone cist with a flat stone bottom and cover and small stones used for the walls contained a cremation in a beaker.

Excavators have been reluctant to put dates to their finds and one can understand why, carbon dating being expensive.

The most common other indications of early occupation must be the presence of flint tools and the chips and cores of the flints from which they were fashioned. Groups of these have been found at many places, chiefly down the Rhinns, with a major Neolithic occupation site at Bolsay on the slope of Beinn Tart a' Mhill and also amongst the sand dunes at Sanaig and Sanaigmore where they are accompanied by large quantities of heat shattered stones, often called pot boilers, from primitive fires. There is no natural flint in Islay so from where did the inhabitants obtain the great quantity of nodules they would require from which to make their tools? It seems unlikely that much was imported, but a walk on the shores of the west coast of the island will discover many pebbles of flint amongst the others, and they vary in size from very small ones, too small to use, to the occasional large one bigger than the largest grapefruit. It has been suggested that these water worn stones have been brought by the tides from Mull or Ireland.

Where flint waste is found there are usually hammer stones and perhaps a stone anvil. Hammer stones are easily recognised amongst the other stones on a site as they show pock marks at each end, and often on the smooth sides, where flints have been struck. When a few have been handled it becomes noticeable how well they fit into the hand. Smaller stones about four to six inches long and only an inch wide which have broken ends could easily have been used to knock limpets off rocks. Flint tools are not very easily recognised and relatively few are found on the sites, perhaps the odd scraper here and there. They must have been too valuable to be discarded wantonly. Bronze Age tanged and barbed arrow heads have been found in at least eight places widely distributed over the island and three more of the leaf shape, and it is probable that others found have not been reported. Stoneware tools recorded include three Larne picks from Bolsay and one from Sanaig, a plough share from the crannog in Loch Gorm, and a neolithic axe head found at Octomore when trenching for water mains. Many small carved stone balls have been found in Scotland and one of them at Keills. Their purpose is not known. Saddle querns, which are a slab of stone slightly hollow on the surface in which corn can be ground using a large pebble, have been recovered from Ardnave, Kilellan and Manitoba, near Port Ellen.

A square vessel and parts of other domestic articles of wood were found about eight feet down in a peat moss at Strathmore, near Gruinart, and bones of a fifteen years old girl and a cow horn were turned up by the same peat diggers.

J. F. Campbell tells of sticks with sharpened ends which had been burnt and hardened in a fire and said he had seen one of them found in a moss, and writes "They used to throw them from them, and could aim exceedingly with them, and they could drive through a man. They used to have a bundle with them on their shoulders, and a bundle in their oxters." In his "Tales of the West Highlands" he mentions the discovery of combs and brooches of a peculiar form . . . similar brooches are commonly found in Denmark . . . and I own a pair found in an old grave in Islay, together with an amber bead. He also knew of the discovery of gold rings and chains. A small talismanic gold brooch of about 1300 AD was found. Anderson in "Scotland in Pagan Times" tells of 36 gold annular armlets, all melted except one, which were found at Coull.

A leaf shaped bronze sword was found at Leannan Buidhie, Coillabus, on the Oa and a small bronze vessel, perhaps a lachrimatory, four ounces in weight, in the chapel on Texa island.

One can sometimes learn something about the population from a study of coins which have been recovered but perhaps not much in Islay. An old market stance will yield comparatively recent ones such as pennies and groats from about the time of William IV. A roman coin belonging to the fourth year of the reign of Diocletian, AD 287, was found on an island in Finlaggan Loch and one wonders how it got there. Perhaps it was brought in by a refugee from the persecution of the Catholic church about that time, when thousands of British communicants, including the bishops of York and Carlisle, perished. A hoard of Anglo-Saxon pennies in silver was found on the farm of Machrie, Kildalton, in 1850. "A small part," 90 entire pennies and a few fragments, was recovered by the Scottish Exchequer and were mostly from the reign of Eadgar with others from Athelstan, Edmund, Eodred and Eadwig. There were also four lumps of silver apparently intended for circulation. Eadgar reigned from 959 to 975.

Found hidden in a cist at Ballynaughton were 74 coins, the latest of which was an Elizabeth issue before 1561, so they must have been deposited in the early part of her reign.

A hoard at Ardnave may have been hidden at the time of the Civil War, between 1638 and 1650 and certainly after 1640. There were at least 81 coins and included one Edward VI shilling, 23 Elizabeth shillings, 17 of James I, some shillings and half-crowns of Charles I but no Scottish coins. 30 were foreign, mostly Spanish. They were the main large size money circulating here during the 17th century. Many more single coins must have been found and have not been recorded.

Major excavations have been done at Kilellan and Ardnave and a much smaller one at Sanaigmore. At Kilellan the area examined so far is only a part of a much more extensive settlement and there is certainly a lot still to be discovered. Amongst the artefacts recorded are a plain bronze pin and a jewelled pin, four arrow heads, two saddle querns, large quantities of Early Bronze Age flint and pot sherds which would indicate more than twenty-five decorated shoulder vases and nine food vessels. The date of occupation would seem to be between 1500 and 2000 BC. The lack of fish remains and the presence of bones of domestic animals suggests that food supply was no problem.

At Ardnave, towards the Point, NR289745, a dig revealed late Neolithic and Early Bronze Age occupation. A small house, oval in shape, was found to be within an earlier and larger stone-built structure dug into sand-dunes; beneath the floor there was a complex of post holes. Subsequent occupation was represented by a large midden with a considerable amount of pottery. A stone hearth, possibly of the Iron Age, about 200 AD, was found quite close and the adjacent midden contained many remains of bones and deer antlers. In places where the sand has completely blown away there are patches of primitive ploughing and a complex of the remains of stone walls. Not far from the hearth a rosette headed silvered bronze pin was picked up and at this site two Viking bronze pins and parts of a bronze buckle.

A little to the east of Ardnave Loch a round house was excavated, the wall of which lay against the edge of a foundation cut in the dune, was skilfully constructed of upright slabs interspersed with thin dry stone panels of water worn pebbles. A bone needle, some animal bones and a few sherds of pottery were found here.

On Borichill Mor, NR307652, a horse shoe shaped burnt patch was found and dated to about 1745 BC. On the west coast of Ardnave, NR272732, a circular structure of twenty-one upright stones has been built partly under overhanging rock; there is nothing else like this on the island.

There are several of those ancient fortified lake dwellings, which we call crannogs, most of them to be found in the northern half of the island, some of them in lochs well up into the hills. These small islands, usually no bigger than would take a house, are connected to the shore by a pavement which is under water when the loch is at normal level, and often the base of the island is reinforced with slabs of stone. The most famous in Islay must be those larger islands in Loch Finlaggan which contained a chapel and a complex of buildings from which the Lords of the Isles ruled their kingdom, the main island being joined to the smaller Council Isle. A small islet at the other end of the loch is supposed to have been a prison.

Islands in Loch Ballygrant and Loch Lossit, which still have substantial building remains, can only be reached by boat. The entrance to one at the east end of Loch Gorm, which can be seen when the water level is low, is rather puzzling and could as easily be the remains of a wall as a path to the island, particularly as when seen in those conditions there appear to be the walls of a square building on the south side about halfway to the island, and if the water level has been raised to improve the fishing it may not be a true crannog. The one in Ardnave Loch which is approached on a visible grass path is often referred to as a burial place and only excavation can provide the answer. The water level in this loch too has probably been artificially raised. There is a crannog in Loch Corr and in several other lochs. That not all have survived is made clear in "The New Guide to Islay," 1900, where it is written that "On a plateau near Laggan farmhouse there was, until recent times, a sheet of fresh water of considerable size called Lochan na Crannaig — which was drained."

A mile to the west of Loch Gorm the road to Gruinart cuts through a settlement at An Sithern of about a dozen round houses which were constructed in the late Bronze Age and which a cursory examination has shown that they were used at least three times. These usually circular or oval grass covered wall foundations occur all over the island and vary in size from about ten feet to forty feet in diameter and can be found alone or in small groups. Often there would seem to be a smaller round structure at the side of the entrance. Some of the small single ones are referred to as burial places but probably represent a dwelling; those in the hills being the remains of summer sheilings.

There are other groups of these huts on the north face of Beinn Tart a Mhill. Cnoc Grianail, Kilellan where some are oval, and from the air one can see a group behind Bridgend. Some would seem to be associated with duns, there being three in the Dun Finn area, a large one at Dun Bhoreraig, some to be seen from the fort in the field below the steep rock face of Dun Nosbridge, and one of fifteen feet across at Trudernish. It is recounted in local folklore that the humps by the chapel at Kilchiaran Bay are the remains of the huts of St. Columba's disciples and possibly the round houses near Kilbride, Keills and Achnaclaiche were associated with the chapels there.

Water supply would be important for both man and beast and many remains are not far from streams such as those near Lossit burn, Kintour river, and Duich river. Many are near fresh water lochs throughout the island as at Loch nan Cadham, Loch Iaran, Glenastle, Loch Fada where there are at least two at Mullach Dubh, Loch Leathan, Loch Kinnabus and Loch Solum, which makes one again think of summer pastures.

Many more are near the sea, Lossit Point, the Ard at Port Ellen, Bolsa and Glean Truath, Aros Bay and Kilchoman Point. There are many others as at Calumkill Lyrabus and Carrabus, Borraichill Mhor, Knoclearach and Ballygrant and the area between Bruichladdich and the west coast.

A dun should be thought of as a fortified dwelling. Those in Islay range from a very simple wall, which at one time perhaps had wood stakes on it, built to enclose a headland and had a narrow entrance at the steepest part, to a substantial hill fort like Borraichill Mhor which encloses a considerable area.

The early inhabitants had to go where there was grass for their animals to feed on and this mobile existence dictated that the home was some form of tent. As agricultural methods improved and the dwelling could be more permanent the tent was made with stone and as we have shown there are the remains of such hut circles in a number of places. As people acquired wealth in the form of goods or animals, protection from robbers became necessary. Perhaps the most secure places were natural or man made islands in lochs, which we call crannogs.

A simple home for a single family was often made on a small rock outcrop which was sheer on three sides and from which an approaching enemy could easily be seen and easily ejected, and such can be found at Dun Finn in Kildalton and at Rockside where a sherd of cordon decorated Iron Age pottery was found. There are several where headlands with steep sides reaching down to the sea just have a wall across the neck. The most spectacular of these is Dun Athad on the Oa and a smaller one at Octofad. They are the most common type and usually marked on the maps as "an dun."

The next development was of those which required a larger number of people to build them and became corporate activities and into which the community cattle and goods could be taken and defended. A good example of this kind is at Borraichill Mhòr, in Kildalton, where a drystone wall encloses a plateau.

A very different type is found at Dun Nosebridge and Dun Guaidbre which are of similar design and are both built on a hill with precipitous rock on the south side. Dun Guaidbre has the lines of the foundation of a building visible on the top. The defences are a series of trenches with high stone and turf earthworks in between. It is perhaps significant that both have Norse names.

The hill fort at Dun Bhorairaig at Dunlossit would seem to have been a broch from the description of it by Thomas Pennant in 1772, but it suffered some reconstruction in Medieval times, it has been suggested to turn it into a lookout, which the magnificent view of the whole of the Sound of Islay would support. Pennant wrote "On the summit is a Danish fort, of a circular form, at present about fourteen feet high, formed of excellent masonry, but without mortar; the walls are twelve feet thick, and within their very thickness is a gallery extending all round. . . ."

The dun at Trudernish is exceptional in that it shows signs of vitrification. These forts were built of stone tied together with wood beams which when set on fire generated sufficient heat to fuse or "vitrify" the stones.

At Dunyveg there is a castle built on a rock almost surrounded by the sea and possibly on the site of a much older dun, but this important Macdonald stronghold is not of the period we are considering.

Surely one of the most curious things ever written about Islay must be by J. Brownlee in a paper "On the Probability that the Distribution of Illegitimacy in the British Isles depends on Survival of Custom from Definite Racial Invasions" (Man, no 119. 1926) in which he says "There are twenty hill forts in Islay and in Jura none; the corresponding rates of illegitimacy are 15% and 5% respectively."

Life in Islay before the Twentieth Century

TO find out how people in Islay lived in olden times and how their style of life differred from that in the other islands is of absorbing interest. As the result of excavations a certain amount has been discovered about life in the pre-historic era, and much has been published. A little is known about the way the duns and the chapels with their carved slabs were used in medieval times but hardly anything about how they regarded the earlier standing stones. We can be fairly certain that the lives of most of the people were dominated by the need to provide the means of subsistence and somewhere to shelter. The limited availability of materials for building and the primitive methods of construction meant that the houses lasted only about a generation and were often rebuilt and frequently added to as the family increased. The remains of sheilings tell us something about the pattern of agriculture and the temporary removal of the people in summer to tend their cattle in the hills. However, evidence of the activities of the population is fragmentary and of uncertain nature.

In the numerous "guides" which have been published over the years the entries are almost always short as in the many editions of Black or Baedeker, often copied, give a general description of the island and tell nothing about the way the people lived. A very early one is by Donald Munro, Dean of the Isles, who travelled through them and in 1594 published a "Description of the Western Isles" which is almost literally just that, with a full list of the small islands round the coast, but an edition by R. W. Munro in 1961 after a further manuscript had been found gives a description of Finlaggan, a photograph not previously published and a list of those who constituted the council of the Lords of the Isles. Munro tells of dogs which were trained to kill seals on the sandy banks of Loch Gruinart, and writes of Bowmore "Pollmair in Irish, and in English the meekle pool." In "The Highlands and Hebrides in 1786" John Knox (not the reformer) hardly mentions Islay. The author of "The New Universal Gazetteer," the second edition of which was published in Edinburgh in 1796, gives only a very short piece, as might be expected, but tells us "There is only one harbour, named Lochindale, in the whole island" and says a "Fair is held on May 18th."

"The Traveller's Guide to Scotland and its Islands" — no author given — in the fifth edition published in 1811, has a brief entry about Ila which is said to labour under the "disadvantage of a great scarcity of wood" and "a considerable quantity of flax is raised here, which is spun by the women;, there are lead mines worked in three different places." Nicholas Carlisle in the two volumes of "A Topographical Dictionary of Scotland," published in 1813, mentions the proposal to build a road to Portnahaven. In volume two of "The Glasgow Geography" of 1825 we are told in the short entry that "wheat is also raised in considerable quantity" and that about 3000 head of black cattle are sold annually. Another "Topographical Dictionary," this time by David Webster, published two years later is largely dependant on Pennant.

Islay is mentioned in a very short description in "Lumsden & Sons Steamboat Companion or Strangers' Guide to the Western Isles and Highlands of Scotland" 1829, but not in the edition of 1820. The steam vessels plying to the island are mentioned.

George and Peter Anderson tell a little more in their "Guide to the Highlands and Islands of Scotland" (London 1834) but still little about the people. They write of "Moille of Keann-outh, or Mull of Oe" and say they found a cheerful and commodious hotel at Port Askaig "nestled securely among well-grown trees." There is a history of the Macdonalds, Finlaggan, and their castles, of Dun Borreraig it is said "as usual there is a gallery in the midst of the walls." One cannot agree with them that in the graveyard at Kildalton there "are two large, but clumsily sculptured stone crosses." They report that "the present proprietor of Islay can use the rare boast of having a proportion of his family plate manufactured from silver found on his own domains." "Ardnave, a handsome residence, beyond Sanaig, is the birth-place, we believe, at least the paternal residence, of Miss Campbell, lady of Polignac, late Prime Minister of France."

The information in the series of guides by J. Watson Lyall which begin in 1873 is mostly about the shootings and fishings. In the third and thoroughly revised edition in the same year of the famous series of Murray guides in the "Handbook for Travellers in Scotland" there is only a short note on Islay.

John Marius Wilson's "The Imperial Gazetteer of Scotland" (Edinburgh 1882) and Cassell's "Gazetteer of Great Britain and Ireland" (London 1896) have short entries largely copied — and often inaccurate — and Cassell repeats the "Two rude sculptured crosses at Kildalton."

There are sections on Islay in many of the piloting and sailing directions for Scotland, and specialist publications about the geology and the minerals, which were published in the 19th century, none of which tells us about the inhabitants. It is not until the turn of the century that what is probably the best guide to Islay was published. The Reverend J. G. MacNeill published his "New Guide to Islay" in 1900 and here we have a book about Islay only, written by an Ileach. He refers to customs in his school days such as the keeping of the Day of the Festival of Bridget, when they took to school a few silver coins as an offering to the teacher, and the boy and girl who took most were called the King and the Queen of the school for a year. He was minister at Portnahaven for ten years. When describing tours of the island he gives the names of the farms, many of which are now just piles of stones, and who occupied them. He makes a special point of mentioning the people who were born in those homes and what became of them, particularly if they achieved fame later in life. He tells stories such as how his grandfather shot at a flock of wild geese from the back of his pony, which took fright, threw him and he broke an arm which had to be amputated, and as a boy the tumulus where the arm was buried was pointed out to him. The list of the founders of Port Ellen in 1821 and their occupations and place of residence which he gives is of great interest.

A little more information can be found in the reports of the "tourists," but as Murray's Guide says, "Islay is seldom visited by tourists, who usually follow the route through the Crinan Canal." We must be grateful to those who did visit the island and for ever regret that it was not included in Dr. Johnson's itinerary.

"A Description of the Western Islands of Scotland" written by Martin Martin — who was a doctor in Skye — was published in 1703 and mentions Finlaggan, the mines, forts, caves, the well that moved itself here from Colonsay, and gives a list of churches, but tells little about the way of life.

I have not been able to examine a copy of the rare "The Tourist's Guide to Islay, the Queen of the Hebrides, with Directory of the Island and Descriptive Excursions to all Parts thereof" which was published by Wilson & M'Cormick in Glasgow, about 1881 and which was probably written by Robert Oliphant who is listed in the Directory as "accountant, Bowmore." This is probably worth study.

The Reverend Dr. John Walker was sent by the Commissioners of Annexed Estates to visit and report on the state of the Hebrides, and, being a prominent naturalist "to examine the natural histories of these countries."

The Society for the Propagation of Christian Knowledge asked him to report on the work of its schools at the same time. He finished his report to them in 1765 but the Commissioners did not get theirs until 1771, and a further expedition in that year produced another report for S.P.C.K. Walker's "Report on the Hebrides in 1764 & 1771" can be read with advantage in the edition by Margaret M. McKay published in 1980. In June 1764 he was inspecting the S.P.C.K. school at Kilchoman and of the island in general writes "Among the children the Measles are peculiarly mortal. The small Pox are less hurtful than in the other islands." He records that "Ila sent to the Army and Navy during the late war 500 men." He says that there is not any coal in Ila, but to this day there are those who say that some coal was found at Daill and used by a blacksmith at Bridgend, although there is no evidence from where this was obtained. On the north side of the River Sorn, by the top dam of the wool mill pool, there are amongst the trees the remains of a village called Workington. Could this suggest a coal connection? He writes little about the lifestyle of the people but lists many of their occupations.

Thomas Pennant was here the following year and his account of his visit with John Lightfoot, the botanist, which appears in "A Tour in Scotland and a Voyage to the Hebrides in 1772" (Chester 1774) is very important and is much used by later writers. He records a visit to the lead mines, carved stones, caves, Loch Finlaggan, and the duns where his description of the state of Dun Bhorairaig at that time is particularly valuable. He discusses shortly the history of the island, the visit of M. Thurot of the French navy, superstitions, the wild animals, cattle, the health of the people and their houses and includes a delightful drawing of the interior of a weaver's cottage.

John MacCulloch, M.D., who was a geologist, did visit Islay but does not seem to have been impressed. In "A Description of the Western Isles," Volume 2, 1819, he says "places referred to may be specific, without the necessity of having much recourse to the often dissonant Celtic and Scandinavian names by which they are marked. He states that few sheep are reared . . . and those only for domestic consumption. Of the monumental stones he writes "However the knowledge of their general existence may be interesting, there is nothing in them, individually considered, to call for a particular description," and of the islands in the lochs he says "Similar remains, situated in the same manner, are seen at Loch Finlaggan; but none of them present any interest to detain either the painter or the antiquary." In volume IV there is a description of the disembarkation of cattle at Port Askaig by throwing them into the sea to swim ashore. Also in this volume he declares that "at Kildalton, there are two crosses covered with sculpture, yet of clumsy proportions, and without any merit."

An important work which I have not been able to consult is "Sketches of the Coasts and Islands of Scotland and of the Isle of Man" by Charles John Shore, Baron Teignmouth. (London 1836. two volumes).

Some thirty pages in volume two are known to contain an account of everyday life on Islay at the time of the author's visit, and notes on the fishing at Portnahaven are particularly valuable.

Alexander Beith, D.D. with his companions Dr Candlish and Dr McKellar, who were appointed by the General Assembly of the Free Church of Scotland to visit and report on the state of matters throughout the Highlands and Islands, started in Islay and spent their one night with Mr Ramsay at Kildalton. They called on Mr Walter Campbell and in their "A Highland Tour" published in 1845 reported that "at the time of our visit, as we learned afterwards, he was close to the painful discovery which, it was said, was to him as unexpected as it was unwelcome — a discovery of his utter insolvency! "They addressed meetings in Kilmeny and Port Ellen and found the condition of the Free Church to be satisfactory.

J. C. Schetky who describes himself as marine painter in ordinary to Her Majesty has little good to say about Islay in "Sketches of notes of a Cruise in Scotch Waters on board His Grace the Duke of Rutland's Yacht Resolution in the Summer of 1848." There is a drawing of the yacht in the Sound of Islay and he went ashore at Port Askaig and into the house of the ferryman whilst a gig-cart was prepared to drive to "Shawfield on the opposite coast" where the grounds had been much embellished lately. He found trees full of beautiful moss roses, red, white and yellow, which showed what can be done to make the desert smile." But I do not like to say much about Islay; let us therefore remount our primitive carriage."

C. F. Gordon Cumming's "In the Hebrides" is a wordy and repetitive account typical of the era. He started his tour in Cantyre and only saw Islay from "the lumbering old coach which still runs between Campbeltown and Tarbert" and dismisses it in a single page of material which he could have taken from anywhere.

R. Kempt in "Convivial Caledonia" (London 1893) gives a short account of the Islay Parliament which he had extracted from an account by Dr D. Anderson in the Scots Magazine of the previous year.

In 1878 The Islay Association printed a report of the proceedings at the Annual General Meeting in Glasgow, which was a special tribute to J. F. Campbell who was then Chairman, and which contains addresses by him, the Reverend Robert Blair, John Ramsay and Professor Blackie, and this is well worth reading.

What a pity that the members of the Napier Commission which was set up in 1883 to enquire into the conditions of the crofters and cottars in the Highlands and Islands were unable to have sittings in Islay; despite pleas for them to visit the island they finished their tour at Tarbert. There could have been so much important material in what has been called "The Domesday Book of the Highlands and Islands."

The Royal Commission (Highlands and Islands) of 1892 spent several days here and the Minutes of Evidence tell about the conditions of crofting, what was grown, yields of the crops, and their stock. The general information gives the size of the holdings, rents and former occupations, from answers given by such people as Dugald Ferguson McFadyen, who at the age of 27, was County Councillor for Kilchoman. Archibald Campbell of Port Ellen tells that they built their own houses on their holdings and "nearly all the householders in the village have one cow." Duncan Campbell Macewan, who for ten years had managed a sheep station in Australia bigger than Islay, had come home and claimed he was the oldest feuer in Bowmore and was one of the few whose feu was for life — "while water runs and grass grows." When the chairman asked "Do you suffer from late harvests?" he was told "Sometimes, not very often." Peter Reid, the Kildalton factor, said about 400 people emigrated from Islay in 1863. The factor of the Islay Estate put in an interesting table of the acreage of the various farms in 1894.

The Statistical Accounts are an important source. In volume 2 of the one edited by Sir John Sinclair — "The Statistical Account of Scotland" (Edinburgh 1794) — the contributors were the Reverend John M'Leish minister at Kilchoman, the Reverend Archibald Robertson at Kildalton and the Reverend John Murdoch of Kilarrow and Kilmeny. In their account they tell how in one season a surgeon inoculated more than 800 children against the small pox "very few of whom died." The wild animals included "sea and land barnicles." There were about 800 black cattle sold annually from Kilchoman parish alone, at an average price of £3 15s 0d; the farmers plough with four horses, flax was an important crop throughout the island. There are descriptions of Dun-Naomhaig and Dun-Aidh, of the castle in Loch Gorm it is said "its bastions are all entire," which was also the state of the chapels. It was "about a century since public worship was performed in Kildalton church. This island has a liberty of brewing whisky without being under the necessity of paying the usual excise duty to the Government."

A much fuller account is in "The New Statistical Account of Scotland" volume VII (1844) when the contributors were the Reverend Archibald MacTavish of Kildalton, the Reverend Alexander Stewart of Kilarrow and the Reverend Alexander Cameron of Kilchoman of which he was lately minister. He does not seem to have liked the personal and domestic habits of his former parishioners and also says "a dislike to continuous work prevails extensively among the working class" and "persons who live temporately have attained a good old age." Besides the parochial school there was one supported by the Society for Propagation of Christian Knowledge, one by the Edinburgh Gaelic School Society and six "taught by persons on their own adventure." The decline of the flax trade is mentioned. "Parochial Registers. These have been kept only since 1822. For several years a register of marriages and baptisms was regularly kept; but since the Parliamentry Churches, with the districts annexed, were erected into parishes quoad sacra, the minister at Portnahaven baptizes and marries without having the names of the parties entered in the parish register." An interesting entry by the Kildalton minister relates that "The only animals which formerly existed in the parish, but are now extinct, are red-deer and foxes." He says that "there are eleven schools in the parish, one parochial, eight unendowed schools and two supported by Societies." The first registers kept were lost, and those now in existence were very irregularly kept, until within the last 50 years. In Kilarrow, a tile works has lately been erected for making drain-tiles; a local Agricultural Society has been established for some years (in fact 1838) and prizes been awarded for the improvement of the breed of black-cattle and sheep, and for the encouragement of green crop husbandry. There is a parochial school in Bowmore, a parliamentary school in Kilmeny parish, two Gaelic Society schools and a female school near Bridgend. There are about a dozen adventure schools, not generally taught throughout the summer and generally inefficient. "There are four parish registers. Marriage register commencing November 15, 1789; Baptism register commencing November 17, 1789; List of poor and state of poor's fund commencing June 13, 1819; Kirk Session minute book commencing March 6, 1823; all regularly kept from respective dates. Anything previous to these dates consisted of mere scraps."

The School Newspaper published fortnightly in Portnahaven in 1894 became "The Rhyns Echo" with number eight and was published weekly. It cost ½d.

In the early numbers there are such diverse items as an account of a tea given for the Baptist children in Port Ellen and the news that Lord Rosebery had succeeded Mr Gladstone as Prime Minister. By number three there was a London correspondent who reported on a visit to a dog show (Crufts) held in the Agricultural Hall, and in number six short articles in the Gaelic about animals. It ran for less than a year. There are a few items of interest, but generally, local news is scarce. In number ten we read that

"The Royal Commission recommended the establishment of telephonic connection between the Rhynns of Islay lighthouse and Bruichladdich at a cost of £330." There were 166 pupils on the roll.

Drink has always been a problem since men discovered how to distil and it is known that there were a great many small stills on the island. In 1883 the Kilarrow Free Church congregation formed a Total Abstinence Society and at the first meeting in January 35 people signed the pledge. They met again in February to hear an address given by someone from the Scottish Temperance League, and in Ballygrant in March when the Chairman gave an address in the Gaelic; seven more joined. Four more were recruited at a meeting in December. They held a Soirée in January of the next year at which 140 were present; tea was made in the manse kitchen. They met in November and not again until December 1885 when at a public meeting at Ballygrant the attendance was rather small "the day being very stormy." The 1886 Soirée in Newton school attracted about 220 people when an agent from the Scottish Temperance League gave a magic lantern show. There was a Soirée in the spring of 1887 and again in 1888 at which "only a few psalms were to be sung, thereby keeping clear of any danger that might creep into our churches by hymns or any other kind of pieces of music." The Annual Social Tea Meetings from 1889 were attended by fewer people and records cease in 1897. Perhaps the meeting in 1896 at which "a choir rendered several hymns which added greatly to the evenings enjoyment" was the last effort to attract more people.

As far as is known, very few people in Islay kept a diary at that time and in those which have survived the entries are short and appear to have been inspired by the prospect of emigration or a return to their native heath by one who had spent many years abroad. Such a one was John Kirk of Bowmore, who kept a diary from the time he went to America in 1852, before the Civil War, and gives a vivid account of his impressions of Canada, Boston, and sweat and slavery in the South, but only a short account of his later years when he had returned to Islay. He died in 1894. John McCorquodale visited Islay, where he was born, to take leave of his relations before emigrating to Canada in 1855 and in the short entry in his diary describes Dun Nosbridge as "the prettiest hill that can be seen anywhere. There also the old folks, as far back as I can recollect, the meeting place of young and old on New Year's Day to play shinty. Here gathered all the neighbours for miles around to celebrate this day, and on occasion a celebrated preacher of the name of Malcom McLaurin occupied the hill above. He was opposed to shinty and the young's enjoyment in general, but they paid no attention to him and the day was spent in the usual lively manner accompanied by bagpipe music and dancing in the open air." And "Here also the Bridge under which on many a Sabbath day I witnessed the Baptists performing the Sacred rite of dipping in the river." He describes the wedding of his brother to Janet Ogilvie at Mulindry.

A source which is denied to those of us who do not have the Gaelic is in the songs of the Islay bards. William Livingston (1818-1870) who apprenticed to a tailor and went from house to house in the course of his work, must have known the people well and written about their hard life.

Occasionally an English translation is given, as of "A Fair Day" and in Thomas Pattison's "The Gaelic Bards," published in 1864, we find—

"But hark, a note of music touched mine ear,
Come, we will trace it up this flight of steps,
Built to an outer wall with clumsy flags,
Whose rough ascent conducts us to the door
now open wide, inviting customers.
Here is a loft, in winter stored with hay,
or corn, or fodder, for the cattle kept,
now swept and fitted for the fiery dance."

There is a description of the home of "The Pious Labourer" who J. C. McNeill tells us lived beside the Loch of the Crannog near Laggan farm, which was later drained and farmed. The Kilchoman bards, Duncan and Charles Macniven, must have written about fellow Ileachs; what has Nigel MacNeill to say in "Neniae" (1872)? It is to be hoped that some day this fruitful field will be explored and the results given to us in English.

Charms and Divination

LAWS against witchcraft were abolished in 1736 but long after that date Church courts still tried people suspected of witchcraft. They could no longer hang or burn them but they were expelled from the church and all its sacraments and services, which at that time was a very severe punishment.

It would appear from the Minutes of the Presbytery of Kintyre that no one in Islay was brought before the meeting of the Presbytery after 1702.

In 1697 "The presbytery being informed by the minister and ruling elder of Kilvarow that Janet NcKalman in Brockachach, Angus Brown in Scarabus, John McVurich in Achtawilling and Milcolm McIllvoil in Grundart doe use charms and divination The Presbytery appoint Allan McDugald their officer to summond them to the next dyet of the Presbytery at Kilchoman. Session 2 da. Sed ut supra. "Allan McDugald presbytery officer reports he could not find Janet NcCalman having no constant residence. The presbytery appoints the church officers of the respective parishes to make inquiry for her and to summond her to the succeeding dyets of the presbytery to be held in the isle. Milcolm MvIllvoil in Grundart alledged charmer being called, compeared not. The presbytery appoint Parick McCalman, Bedle of this parish, to summond him pro secundo to the next dyet. In regard Angus Brown, John McVurich are in the parish of Kilvarow the presbytery refers them till the next dyet therein."

November 1697. "Milcolm McIllvoil being called compeared and confessed he practised a charm with a string and some words he spoke within the compass of the string for the rickets possession and any other sudden distemper which he did practice by putting a lint thread to his breath and repeating the following words within the compass of it, viz. 'Cuirim cumerih dhia umid sluagh dall tharrid do vho gach gabhadh Sosgeul dhia na grais o mullach gu lar unid ga ghradhich na fire thu i na millidh na mhuaih thu.' (I put the protection of God around you, a blind host over you, to protect you from every danger. The Gospel of the God of Grace from top to ground over you. May the men love you, and may the women do you no harm.) And asserts that he did it ignorantly not knowing there was any evil in it, and after the several members of the presbytery had dealt with him and endeavoured to convince him of the sinfulness of the said practice he seemed to dislike the practice of the charm and judicially promised to forbear it for the future. The presbyterie taking the heignanse-ness of the crime in their consideration doe in odium fanti at terrorum allis appoint Mr. David Sympson his parish minister publickly to rebuke him for it before the congregation and then to take occasion to admonish the people against the evil of such practices and they recommend to the Baillie of Ila to put the acts of parliament against charmers in execution. Angus Brown in Scarabus alledged charmer being summoned and called compeared not. The Presbytery appoints the beadle of the parish to summond him pro secundo. John McVurich in Octovuillin alledged diviner being summoned and called compeared not. The Presbytery appoints the beadle to summond him pro secundo again nixt being the 13th. instant."

11th. November. "In regard Janet NcCalman charmer hath not constant place of residence nor could be found by several church officers. The presbytery appoints Mr Dugald Campbell to summond the said Janet from the pupil after sermon on Saturday next."

16th. November. "John McVurich, alledged diviner, being summond and not compeared recommended him to the session of Kilarrow to processe him for the same. Compeared Janet NcCalman alledged charmer and being questioned as to her using of charms confessed that she used one charm for Causing Cows bull (called eelis dhair) which she practices by expressing some words over water and that she gave it particularly to one NcAbhrionid in Balulise. The presbyterie after dealing with her and finding her grossly ignorant recommends to Mr David Simpson her minister to instruct her privately and afterwards to rebuke her publickly.

Compeared Angus Brown in Scarbus and confessed he practiced a charme by uttering some words with a string he held to his mouth which string was to be bound about the hand of the sick person. The presb. after serious dealing with him to convince him of the evil of the said practice, and after receiving his promise judicially not to practice it any more appoints him to be publickly rebuked before the congregation by his parish minister."

Jan. 1702. "Compeared John Campbell, charmer, and being interrogated if he had practiced a charme att Port Askaig with a bible and a key, reading some verses in the fiftieth psalm in order to find out theft, did acknowledge the said charme. The presbytery having dealt with him to bring him to the conviction of the evil of the said practice did appoynt him to be publickly rebuked two several Lord's days in the Kirk of Kilarrow and Kilmeny."

William Macdonald in his "Sketches of Islay" 1850 writes, "Islay had also its wizards and witches, and their charms and amulets were, till of late, very much dreaded by the generality of the people. These impostors reaped rich and abundant harvest among their dupes; but by means of the wholesome instructions of the Gospel, superstition is fast giving way. A male and a female who stood at the head of the profession have died lately, and it is supposed their places shall not be filled."

AMULETS

THOMAS PENNANT in his "Tour in Scotland" 1772 writes, "A present was made me of a clach clun ceilach, or cock-knee stone, believed to be obtained out of that part of the bird; but I have unluckily forgotten its virtues. Not so with the clach crubain, which is to cure all pains in the joints. It is to be presumed both these amulets have been enchanted; for the first very much resembles a common pebble; the other is that species of fossil shell called Gryphites.

"I was also favoured with several of the nuts, commonly called Molucca beans, which are frequently found on the western shores of this and others of the Hebrides. They are the seed of the Dolichos urens, Guilandina Bonduc. G. Bonducetta, and mimosa scandens of Linnaeus, natives of Jamaica. The fifth is a seed called by Bauhin, fructus exot; obicularis sulcis nervisque quatuor, whose place is unknown. The four first grow in quantities on the steep banks of the rivers in Jamaica, and are generally supposed to drop into the water, and to be carried into the sea; from thence, by tides and currents, and the predominency of the East wind, to be forced through the gulf of Florida, into the North-American ocean, in the same manner as the Saragosso, a plant growing on the rocks of the seas of Jamaica. When arrived in that part of the Atlantic, they fall in with the Westerly winds, which generally blow two-thirds of the year in that tract; which may help to convey them to the shores of the Hebrides and Orkneys. I was for resolving this phenomenon into ship-wrecks, and supposing that they might have been flung on these coasts out of some unhappy vessels; but this solution of mine is absolutely denied, from the frequency and regularity of the appearance of these seeds."

A visitor brought two of these which he had found on the shore near Saligo Bay in the summer of 1980, for me to identify.

It is strange that I can find no reference to these beans in Peggy Earl's "Tales of Islay" because it was she who told me that they were sometimes called "fairy eggs" and that some of the more wealthy people had them set in silver mounts to wear round their necks.

"Evil Eye in the Western Highlands" by R. C. MacLagan, M.D., London 1902 but reprinted by E.P. Publishing in 1972, contains a great many Islay references.

The Islay Parliament 1718-1843

NO one can have done more for the historian studying Islay than Mrs Lucy Ramsay who had "The Book of Islay" and "The Stent Book & Acts of the Bailliary of Islay"prepared for publication. Two hundred and fifty copies of each were printed privately, about fifty were presented to friends and libraries and the remainder lost in a fire at a warehouse in Glasgow.

At the time when these minutes were recorded the island was the property of the Campbells of Calder to whom it had been granted by Royal charter in 1621 for an annual payment of 9000 merks Scots, or about £500 sterling, to the Crown. "The Baillie and Gentlemen of Islay" and later "The Gentlemen, Fewers, Heretors, Tacksmen of Islay" met, at first twice a year and later annually, to consider what needed to be spent and how it was to be raised. There is no indication how they decided what had to be paid for by the Stent but the total liability was divided amongst 132 quarter lands.

The first entry in the book (it is not known whether this is the first book) is "Killerow, July 17th 1718. Then Stented the June and September Cess, and is only — The King's part, £325.0.0 Scots money. Which, being divided amongst 132 quarter lands, each share £2:9:4. They met again in November and stented for The King's part

and stented for The King's part	325 0 0	
The Chyrurgion fees	40 0 0	
Kildaltan Schoolmaster's sellery	12 10 8	
To repairing of the meeting-house at Lagavullin	20 0 0	
To Collectors of the cess their selleries	66 13 4	
To purchassing of the timber and house lately possessed by Lagganlochan, standing on the lands of Knockans, conforme to bill of comprizmt thereof	53 0 0	517 4 0

Which, being divided amongst 132 quarter lands, each share is 3:19:4.

The following items of particular interest are extracted.

1719 for building an Schoolhouse for Killdaltan parish	20 0 0
1721 to the purchassing of the Communion Eliments	83 14 0
to the expences of an Express sent out to Mr. Anderson in Edinr. annent the Plague in Winter last,	12 0 0
to Abarew Innis for his services during that time	6 0 0
to harleing etc of the Schoolhouse of Killerow	6 0 0
1727 ffor the building of the Kirk of Kilnachtane	147:8:0
1728 ffor Schools in Islay	13:6:8

A note that the next stent is to pay £5 sterling to Allexr. McMillen, writer at Edin. for Defending the Country against the Sub penas Served against them for Candle and Leather. These were duties on the tanning of leather and making of candles.

1730 For the fraught and Expences of Carying Lintseed 18:6:0

1730 "That there is a new church to be builded in Killdaltane parish, and alsoe the churches of Killearow & Kilchoman to be repaird" For building and repairing churches in Islay 300:0:0
"That the building of the Church of Lagwilline will at leist cost £100 Ster., of which soume the proprietor hase agreed to pay £50 Ster." They agree to raise the other £50.

1731 The Commissioners of Supply imposed a charge of £32 Scots. for mending the highways in the Shire of Argyll.

1740 A new item appears "The Compearance money is £104:12:0. this was for ffarqhuard Campbell, the Clerk.

1745 "The Gentlemen befrementd. taking to Consideration That there are a great deal thefts Committed in this Country Doe to prevent & Discover the samen come to the following Resolutions, That The Chamberlain of Kildaltan & Some of the princl. Gentlemen in that parish Conveen & Appoint such of their Number as they see proper in rexive Districts to make a search twice a week throwout sd. Parish." Here follows the appointments for the various districts. "That they secure every person in whose family or possession Stolen goods are found, & Commit them to Killarow Prison, & secure all their Effects, and that they Call for Assistants, & such as refuse to report the same, who are to be fyned in Ten pund for each refusal & Deemed Dishonest."

The old Town Hall, once a Sheriff Court, Bowmore.

1750 To Linnine for Communion table for both parishes 12:0:0. "The Surveyers and Overseers of Ilay Appoint that the roads be Wrought on this Year. On the Last thursday, fryday & Saturday of this moneth, as follows: — The People of Kildaltan to work where they Left off Last year." And so on for the whole island.

1751 "And in regaird Shawfield was in use to ffurnish three setts of News papers for this Country, till of Late that the same was withdrawn, And that at first Erecting of the post office here, Shawfield agreed to Continow the same with us for our Encouragement in keeping up of a post. Therefore its now recomended to Skipnish to represent this to Shawfield, And that unless the three sets of News papers be Continowd by him to us, That the post Drops. . . ."

1754 In 1750 a shilling sterling was levied for each quarter land for building a dyke about the Church yard of Killarow but it was not yet finished.

There is a list of the Quarter Lands in Killarow parish.

1760 "The Meeting Appoints that Six days in harvest be Imployed in Working on the Roads of Islay, . . . That the Inhabitants of Ballulve, Ballighiline, Moalrish, Persabus, & Kile, wt. Carnbeg, work on the Quey & ffank of Portaskog . . ."

1762 "To be payd for killing the Dog that Destroys the Sheep of the Country 3:3:0

1769 "It is agreed that a sufficient Dyke be built about the Church Yard of Killarow, on such Lyne as Shawfield with the Concurrence of Colin Campbell, Carnbeg, Doctor Robertson, & Lagganlochan shall direct And the Expence thereof to be payd out of the overplus sum stented as King's Cess, above what ought to be stented as King's Cess for this year and Last year."

"It is settled now with David Simson, Mercht. in Ilay, That he Continue the packquet to run to & from Tarbet as Usuall. On the same Conditions yearly as she was keepd the two Last years, He being obliged to ffit her up without Loss of time sufficient in Sails, Rigging & others needfull, And to raise her two planks in the Upper Work, And that the Cabine be raised Accordingly, And that there bees four Beds in said Cabine properly furnished."

At many subsequent meetings there are regulations laid down for the conduct of the Pacquet, and a committee appointed to see that they were conformed to.

1771 "This meeting also agreed That the sum of one shilling & sixpence Sterling be levied on each Quarter Land towards payment of Expences of a Dyke arround the Burial place in Kilchoman."

1772 To be payed to William Mitchell for Caping the Church yard Dyke of Killarow. 1:3:0

Expences of the Gate to the Church yard Dyke of Killw., being Duncan McLachlan & the Smith's charges, 2:18:11.

1773 "To be levied for finishing the Church yeard Dyke of Kilchoman and the Remainder thereof to be applied towards building the Church yeard Dyke of Kildalton with future collections, till the same be Completed.

1774 "To William Mitchel's Charge for ffree Stone to the Church yeard Dyke at Killarow £1:5: and for Caping the said Dyke £1:1:"

Nothing had been done towards building the Church yard Dyke of Kilchoman.

In September "Mr. John Wodrow, Minister of the Parish of Kildalton, having Represented That the Church of Lagavullin was stripped of many slates, and otherwise much hurt by the Storm, and that it is absolutely necessary That the same be immediately Repaired, otherwise that the Church will become ruinous . . ." £7:4:0 was granted.

1775 "A plan and Estimate of a Church yeard Dyke arround the Kirk of Bowmore, amounting to ffourty four pounds one shilling and seven pence sterling, being produced, which sum Shawfield is to lay out next season, and this meeting stent themselves with the sum of twenty pounds Sterling of the said sum for this year, and agree that the rest of the said sum be stented in following years."

The Collector of the Road Money, his Sallery £2:0:0

To the two thirds of the Road money to be levied & paid with the Cess in terms of the new Act of Parliament £24:13:4

To be paid to John Taylor, waulking miller, for making a Timber Bridge over the water at the Lint Mill £2:0:0.

This Meeting, taking also into Consideration the numbers of Complaints against makers & sellers of yearn in Isla, hereby appoint that a Mercat for yearn shall be held at Bowmore on the first Tuesday of March yearly, and on such other days as they afterwards shall appoint, And hereby ordain the Clerk to make advertisments for the different Parish Kirks. Setting forth That if any yearn is produced at the said Mercat or at any of the Mercats of Isla, the same not being just in number & Length. That such Yearn shall be Confiscatted — And the Partys havers thereof ffined in such sum as the Baillie of Isla shall see Cause. It is also meant that Yearn shall or may be sold on the other Mercat days in Isla, viz — Whity., Lammas, & Hallow day Mercats."

"The meeting also considering that some Complaints are made of the weights & measures of Isla, do appoint . . . a Committee for inspecting & adjusting same."

1776 The Meeting stent themselves with the Expence of Building the Timber Bridge over the water of Duich performed by Hugh McKay £6:0:0. The meeting insist that the Committee for Building the Church yeard Dyke of Kilchoman are to have the same finished on or before the middle of June next.

The meeting Reccommend to Mr. McNiell of Ardnacross to get the Church yeard Dyke of Kildalton finished as soon as possible. .

1777 The meeting having heard the Report of the Committee for

Building the Kirk Yeard Dyke of Kilchoman, do sustain the Reasons . . . for not having the work compleated. . . . The Church Yeard of Kildalton . . . is already partly finished. . . . The Meeting Stent themselves with fifteen shillings sterling being the estimate given for Painting the Church yeard Gate of Kilarow and putting up the Globes on the Pillars of the Gate. . . .

They are of the opinion that a Wooden Bridge on the water of Killarow near the Walk-Mill is very necessary, and should be built as soon as possible and made so sufficient that Horses may pass.

1778 It is reported that the Kirk Yeard of Kilchoman is nearly finished. The meeting recommends the Committee respecting the Lint Miller "to meet with the Lint Miller, and to show him such Evidence as they can recover respecting the weight of fflax in other Countrys — and Endevour to get him to agree to dress & deliver fflax for the same payment and by the same weight, and to report to the next meeting."

For the first time there is "Bill due to Miss Simsons for Entertainment at this Stent £8:10:0.

To Dinner to Gentlemen & Servts.	2: 0:0
9 Dozn & 2 Bottles punch at 9/- Doz	4: 2:6
9 Bottles of Port wine @ 2/6 pr. Bottle	1: 2:6
3 Dozn & 8 Bottles porter	16:0
Cold drams	2:0
Glasses broke 10 @ 6d. each	5:0

1779 "Renews the order on the Committee respecting the ffees of dressing fflax & they to report to the next meeting."

1781 "The Society for Propagating Christian Knowledge having appointed a Schoolmaster for the Parish of Kildaltan, with a Sallary of six pounds sterl., on the Express condition that the Parish should pay him four pound more — Therefore the Parish of Kildaltan are Stented with the said sum. Continued in 1782 & 1783.

1784 "The Meeting considering that there is now no Charity Schoolmaster in the Parish of Kildaltan, and Therefore the four pounds yearly for said Schoolmaster falls, and the Gentlemen of the Parish of Kildaltan having represented that they wish to have a fund for Purchasing Communion Tables & furms, and that four pounds sterl. will be necessary for that purpose, . . . agree to stent themselves for the sd. four pounds for this year. . . ." It being reported to this Meeting that the Peck Measures of the different corners of Islay do not agree in size, & that many of them are deficient of the Legal Standard Measure of this Country-In order to remedy this evil it is recommended that in place of the Heaped Peck commonly used that a streak measure answering exactly to the standard measure of Islay shou'd be substituted in place of the Heap measure, & in order to carry this Resolution into Execution the Meeting do hereby appoint the following Committee . . . it is earnestly recommended to these Gentlemen to have the different Pecks of the different Parishes brought to the proper Streak measure, and to have these pecks Branded with Shawfield's Iron, and this being once done it is recommended to the said Committee to cause publish at the Parish Churches that if any person within their Bounds shall Sell or Buy with any other peck than the Peck so ascertained & stamped, that they shall be Fined at the discretion of the Baron Baillie of Islay. . . ."

"They therefore do appoint that a merket shall be weekly held upon the open Street of Bowmore upon friday, the 1st. to be upon friday the 5th. day of November next, and to be from thenseforth contiunes weekly thereafter . . . and that there may be no fraud in the weight or measure of the different Vivers and commodities Brought for Sale to this weekly merket, the Meeting do hereby appoint Archd. Adair in Bowmore to be Dean of Guild for regulating weights and measures. . . .

1785 Repairs of the Church of Lagivulin. "it is recommended to the said Committee to certify to the Schoolmaster, that he must at his own Expense repair every pane of Glass that shall be broke while he keeps School there."

"The Meeting stented Ten pounds Sterl. for the Bridge built upon the water of Duich," . . . and recommended that "the wood of the Bridge to be paid with Tar and top Covered first with wrought Clay over the Tar and then Graveld, and it is further recommended to Sell the Timber of the old Bridge. . . ."

"The Meeting having considered many Complaints from Caddelton and the other principle Drovers . . . from the want of a proper Fank for Cattle near the ferry place of Portaskaig, and Considering also that sixty or Eighty acres at least of some muir land near the Port will be necessary . . . appoint a Committee to draw up an application to Shawfield, praying he may allot and Inclose a piece of ground. . . ."

It was agreed that ffive pounds should be Stented for Cloathing & Supporting Archd. Campbell, late of Lossit, . . . the Pauper.

1788 "The Meeting having had many Complaints of the Great danger to Travellers in Crossing the Water of Auchacharlich, and that several persons have of late been lost in the water, and considering that a Sufficient Timber Bridge will answer every necessary purpose there, this Meeting" appoints a Committee for erecting the said bridge.

"It being represented to this meeting that part of the Church yard of Kilnaughtan, facing the South E: or the sea is likely to be carried away by the Blowing of Sand and that several Coffins have been exposed" the meeting appoints a Committee to obtain any estimate for banking.

"in Several parts of the Country, they have already established the Herring Gauge Barril filled to the Brim as a proper measure by which Putatoes aught to be bought and sold, and that four fulls of the said Barril shou'd constitute the Boll, but that in other quarters of the Countrey they are in use to Buy and Sell Putatoes by a Creel measure which is very uncertain. The Meeting therefore . . . Establish the Barril Measure over the whole Island of Islay. . . ."

1791 The Gentlemen of the Parish of Kildaltan represent that the Church is much Injured by the Schools being kept therein and that it would be for the General benifit of the Parish to have a School House Built seperate from the Church . . . appoint a Committee for fixing the Stance of the School House and getting the same Built."

". . . the Church Yard of Kilmeny is quite open, never having been Inclosed, & that besides the Indecency thereof, the Grave Stones are much Injured by Horses and Cattle pasturing thereon . . ." ask for an estimate for building a stone wall.

1792 It being Represented to this Meeting that their is unlawful combinations and Meetings held by the Weavers in the Island, particularly in the Parish of Kilchoman, for the purpose of shortening or cutting off the usual measure called the Islay Ell, which has for time Immemorial been the Standard Measure given by the Weavers with every Species of their Manufacture, and for reducing the measure to the English yard, and for continueing the prices for the English yard as high as that for the Islay Ell — This Meeting highly disapprove of such illegal meetings & combinations, and recommend it to the Gentlemen of the difft. districts in Islay to Prosecute before any of his Majestie's Justices of the Peace."

1793 "The Meeting having considered a Petition from Robt. Carrick, Lint Millar, representing the decay'd State of the Timber Bridge at the Lint Mill" . . . agree to the erecting of a new one.

"The Meeting considering that the number of useless Dogs in this Country are a great grievance, and that for many obvious reasons their number should be deminished., and it being also represented that a number of Half Grayhounds very destructive to Hares are kept by Many — This Meeting recommend to the Gentlemen of the different quarters of Islay to Intimate to the people of their neighbourhood that all useless and superflous Dogs are to be killed, and that the owner of any Dog found chasing Sheep or Lambs or running Hares shall be liable for the Damages, and the Meeting also recommend that no dog be seen at Church or other publick Meetings."

1794 Fencing & Enclosing the Churchyard of Kilnaughton. "having seen two Estimates . . . they disapprove of the sd. estimates, as they think the work may be Executed in a much easier and cheaper manner, especially as the gentlemen from the Parish of Kildaltan undertake that the Tennants will lead the stones, build the Baracade at the sea, and furnish the copeing." But in 1796 Mr. John MacDuffie Engages to this Meeting, with Geo. Campbell, Kinnabus, that the Tennants of the Parish will at their own Expence Fence the side next to the sea and see that the other three sides are enclosed by contract within twelve months.

"The Meeting Considering the great Exertions of the Legislature in Surpressing the Distilling of Spirits & the great revenue given up by Ministry for the purpose of providing a sufficiency of Grain for the use of the nation, which in many parts is threaten'd with a Famine, and Considering that great Exertions have already been made in surpressing the Distilling in this Island, This Meeting unanimously Resolve Individually and Collectively to exert themselves in putting a total stop to the said Illegal Practices. . . ."

1798 Repairing Duich Bridge. "recommend earnestly to them to purchase Timber, that may answer the purpose, from the wreck of the Brig stranded on Duich Bay, if she is to be broken up. . . ."

The meeting agree to pay Mr. Hill £6.18.2 for what he has spent on the Fank at Portaskaig, and to open a subscription paper at the May Market for receiving contributions from the Dealers in Cattle.

"This Meeting, with every feeling of humanity for the distressed Sufferers, who have the misfortune to be shipwrecked on the coast of this Island, have to regret that numbers of the Country prople, shaking off all fear of God, or regard to the laws, are in the constant practice against every rule of Christian charity, or hospitality, of resorting in numbers to the shores, where strangers have the Misfortune of being shipwrecked, and that for the sole purpose of plunder; which practice this Meeting hold in the greatest abhorrence, and now declare their disapprobation of; and in order, as much as possible, to remedy this evil, this Meeting not only collectively, but individually, pledge themselves to use their utmost exertions, not only for the preservation of the property of the individuals, who may have the Misfortune to be wrecked on these coasts, but also for bringing to condign punishment all and every such persons as may be found plundering from wrecks:"

1800 A committee is recommended to procure the cheapest Estimates for enclosing the Burying places in Kilmeny & Kilneave with Dry stone walls not Exceeding 3½ feet high with two rows of Fale as Cape.

1801 An estimate of £10:12:6 for enclosing Kilneave was considered too much and was rejected, no estimate was produced for Kilmeny. There was an estimate of £7:1:0 for enclosing Kiels, with a gate, and they recommended that it be done if it did not exceed £6.

"This Meeting having considered an overture of the Kirk Session of Bowmore . . . respecting the procuring of Mortcloths for the better and ordinary Classes of people . . . do hereby agree to Guarrantee to the said Kirk Session, that whatever sum shall be laid out in the purchase of the said Mortcloths, the Princl. sum and Interest shall be reapid to the Session, before they are rendered unfit for use. . . ." The Kirk Treasurer was told to charge "for the best 5/- each time it is used, and at the rate of 2/- each time for the Coarser one."

The meeting stented £10 for the Directors of the Royal Infirmary of Glasgow, "wishing to Contribute for so laudable a Plan," and a like sum next year.

"This Meeting having taken into Consideration the State of the Island as to Grain & provisions, until the next Crop comes on, are of opinion that with economy, there may be neither in the Island, what is sufficient for the Support of the Inhabitants, but if any Grain or putatoes are exported from the Island, that it may endanger a scarcity. . . ." and they are "to use their utmost exertions for preventing any of the Grain of the Island being destroy'd by Illegal Distillers. . . ."

1802 Resumed consideration of the Bridge over the river at Duich, the enclosure of the burying ground at Kilneave and at Kilmeny. The enclosure at Kiels was nearly complete.

1803 "From a statement to this Meeting of the Desertion of the Militia men or non appearance; which they consider as Disgracefull to the Inhabitants of Islay, and the more particularly as the said Militia Regt. is under the Command of the Heir apparent to the Estate of Islay. . . . They hereby resolve to use every mean in their power to Detect the Deserters now presented upon a list. . . ."

"The Meeting Considering that the Island is in a backward state of Cultivation, have Resolved as an Improve ment that each occupier of a 4d. land in Tillage over the whole Island shall sow in the ensuing Spring 2 pecks of Peas & Beans, and for enabling them to have proper Seed they now request that Shawfield will take the trouble of sending a Cargo of Peas & Beans to the Island in proper time. . . ."

1804 It has now been represented to the Meeting that the Town of Bowmore is very much annoy'd by a destructive Crowd of Pigs running up and down the Streets, and that many of the Inhabitants, regardless of Property, keep their Dunghills upon the Streets. This Meeting consider themselves Authorised to order a better Police . . ." and institute fines.

"The Meeting have taken it into Consideration the Complaints which every member of this Meeting have now stated, that their Dykes and Inclosures are very much Damaged and broke down by passengers assuming to themselves a right to take Cross and Short Cuts thro' Inclosures. . . . Find it necessary to check these Inroads. . . ."

1805 The stent includes "The Sum allow'd Mrs. MacMillan, Professed Midwife, for her encouragement to attend & remain in the Island for this year. £5" The repair of the Duich Bridge is still under consideration and it is reported that "the Bridge of Corary is likely to Fail for want of some material repair" and a sum is stented.

"This Meeting having with much regret felt the Inconveniences arising to the Island for the Want of a Jail, wherein Disturbers of the Peace and other Transgressors of the Law might be Confined . . . are of the opinion that Shawfield should be apply'd to, and these Grievances Stated, that he may of course procure the Sherriff's warrant to have a Jail Established. . . ."

"It having been Stated to this Meeting that a regular Ferry from Skiba to Gartbreck would contribute much to the Convenience of Travellers" they agree "to Engage a proper person, who will engage to maintain a proper Ferry Boat ready at all reasonable times to Ferry passengers. . . ."

1806 "This Meeting having taken into Consideration the enormous amount of the Bill of Entertainment ("The Bill at MacTaggart's £16"), Resolve that the following rules shall be attended to in future, viz. That for each Guest Setting at Table, the Landlord shall allow & produce a half Bottle of wine and a Bottle of Punch — a Bottle of Brandy to the whole Company — with small Beer — that the Landlord shall charge for each Sitting to Dinner at the rate of 3/-, that the Servants shall be Limited to a half mutskin of Whisky. . . ."

Little seems to have been done to repair the various bridges and now, "Ballinaby having presented to this Meeting an Estimate of a Bridge to be built upon the water of Saligo. . . . This Meeting do hereby Stent themselves in the sum of £15."

"This Meeting being informed that Cart Drivers are very inattentive as to their Conduct upon the road with Carts — It is now recommended that all Travellers upon the road shall take to the Left in all situations, and that when a Traveller upon the road shall loose a shew of his horse, the Parochial Blacksmith shall be obliged to give preference to the Traveller."

1807 "The Meeting having revised the Consideration of last year's resolution respecting the Restriction as to the Liquor . . . now think that this restriction is not necessary . . . the Constables shall also be prohibited from Eating or Drinking at the Expence of the Publick."

1808 "It having been Represented to this Meeting that the Fund for raising the Militia men by a Publick Box was found Inadequate to raise the men, of course the Funds were found deficient by one Hundered and eight pounds 14/- . . . this Meeting consider themselves bound to advance upon this Deficiency the one half . . . The Heritors they conceive will pay the other half. . . ." "The Meeting Judge it proper and Expedient to appoint a Committee to investigate into the Deficiency in Militia Funds.'

1809 The Meeting having understood that great confusion and Litigation arises from the measure in Barley Deliver'd at the Different periods — . . . now order henceforth the measure in Barley shall be sixteen pecks of the Islay measure at all seasons. . . ."

"The Meeting considering that the old channel at the end of the Iron Bridge continues to annoy the Traveller . . . contract for Erecting a sufficient Causway over the said old channel."

1811 "It being known to this Meeting that two Parochial Schoolhouses are upon the way of being finished at Kilchoman and Kilmeny, and that it is proposed to build a third schoolhouse at Kildalton . . . stent themselves in the sum of £70."

"It is stated to this Meeting that the Lint Miln is keep'd in very bad order, and that it is insufficient to manufacture the Lint of the Parish independent of the Lint of the whole Island. This Meeting consider this a great hardship, Lint being a staple article of the Island — they therefore wish Shawfield may have the Goodness to order matters upon such a footing as to enable his Tenantry to put their manufacture to the best avail."

1812 "It is proposed that the Clergymen of the Island shall . . . convene the poor of their respective Parishes, & to such as they find needy, to issue a Ticket of his or her name & Parish Written thereon, who only should be served as the Poor, & impostures excluded — It is Represented to this Meeting that a number of Beggars keep dogs at home and abroad — . . . and as Scarcity is apprehended, it is considered proper that every person should this year Discharge every unnecessary Dog. . . ."

1814 "This Meeting knowing that they are Bound to pay the Carriage of the articles required for building the Church of Kildaltan. ... Stent the Parish of Kildaltan in the ascertained sum...."

"It being stated to this Meeting that the Water of A-ruagh under Kilchoman House is at present impassable — and a total obstruction to Travelling until a Bridge is erected — ... Stent themselves in the sum of thirty pounds ... in the Expectation that Shawfield will ... contribute towards finishing it...."

1815 "The Meeting concieving it to be highly usefull that the Road from Portaskaig should be rendered complete, do willingly Stent themselves in the sum here stated." (£20).

1816 "The meeting have now to relieve Shawfield of the sums now payble. to the Schools in Islay, charge themselves with the said sum, as a provision for four Schoolmasters, at the rate of £16:13:4 Sterl. to each."

"The meeting having considered the application of the Schoolmaster of Kildaltan for the payment of the sum he expended upon building his House — they have examined said accot. — and reprobate the conduct of the Schoolmaster in carrying on a work of such magnitude without authority — and they refuse to countenance such conduct...."

1817 "The Meeting impressd, with the distress of the Tenantry of the Island from the reduced state of the Price of Black Cattle &c.; conceive it proper and necessary to make application to Shawfield and his Trustees for a reduction of Rent while the times continue so oppressing, but with proper delicacy to this subject they decline making application at Present and till it is ascertained how cattle markets may go in June next....."

"It is now stated that a vast importation of Irish Beggars have already arrived upon the Island, and that others are likely to follow from the misconduct of our own Boatmen — the Community at large are warned to beware of harbouring foreign beggars...."

The accounts include "Patron Jugs procured at Stirling from the Standard there 15:0."

1818 "The Meeting appoint the Islay peck measure to be regulated by the measure obtained from Sterling."

In 1718 the Chyrurgion fees were £40:0:0 Scots. per annum, which in 1751 became £3:6:8 Sterling, and stayed at that for 67 years. And now "The Meeting having given due consideration to the want of a regular and resident Surgeon in the Island, and conceive that such a person is much wanted, and they know that in general the practice and payments to a medical person is inadequate to support him in decency, and altho' a liberal subscription was opened and entered into by individuals still the supply would be scanty and unequal to the support of an educated person and a gentleman. This Meeting know they have no title to impose a Tax upon the Community at large towards this purpose, but they feel it an indispensible duty to express how desirable it would be for the use and service of the inhabitabts of Islay, that a fixed sum in some shape was provided to a deserving and respectable Surgeon, trusting means may be devised for accomplishing this wish."

1820 After all the labour of "obtaining pint and choppin standard measure out of Stirling castle, which have been proven & marked by the Dean of Guild of Stirling as correct, some of members of this meeting ventured to say that these jugs are composed of tin, and easily dimpled, whereas they are composed of the strongest sheet copper tinned within to prevent corrosion. It will be worth while to call upon the asserters to repair to Bridgend to witness the appearance of the jugs, on which they must feel conscious of an irregularity and impropriety of conduct. . . . It is hereby ascertained that nine pints and one choppin of the said Standard measure make a peck, and that sixteen pecks make a Boll."

1821 "This Meeting having given due consideration to various kinds of theft committed in the Island — Resolve to stent themselves in a sum (£20) . . . for the purpose of detecting and prosecuting such persons as may be found guilty of theft."

"This Meeting consider themselves authorised to regulate the practice to be hereafter adopted in Smithies — and direct now that he who comes to the smithy first prepared for work shall have preference in finishing all his work of every kind before any other can pretend to interfere."

1823 "now direct the Collector to pay Twenty pounds Sterling as the sum formerly stented, and to be appropriated for the suppression of thieves — of which sum the Collector will be discharged on paying the same to Mr. McAlpine . . . for his outlay on his dwelling house."

The General Post Office appears in the accounts for the first time. "By 2 years allowance by G.P.O. paid by Niel Currie, Postmr. £10."

1824 "This Meeting being impressed with the utility to the Island by the appointment of a Steamboat to ply in place of the Packet, do unanimously Stent themselves in the sum of one Hundred and ten pounds sterling for this current Year. . . ."

1825 "The Presses of this meeting, as being part owner of the Steam Boat, declines allowing the assessment for the Steam Boat to be charged for this year. This Meeting consider that the sum appropriated for the Steam Boat last year would be best disposed of — by carrying on works of utility to the Island. . . ."

The accounts include payment of £5 each to Dr. Currie and Dr. Hill; and in 1826 £5 to Dr. McKellar also, and £5 each to McEwin, Midwife, Kildalton and Mrs. McMillan, Midwife, Bowmore.

"This Meeting recommend to the Collector to procure from the County town Models of the Imperial Weights and measures, and to put them in the hands of Samuel Lamont, who is appointed to ascertain that all weights and measures within the Island be corrected and marked by the standard."

1827 "Samuel Lamont is instructed by the Justices of the Peace to survey the Baker's stock of Bread occasionally, and weigh their loaves, and report the weight and price of each loaf. . . ."

1830 "The Post Horn made by John McAlister 1:6d."

1834 "The Sum allowed Mr. Colin M'Tavish, Surgeon, this year £36 13 4

Doctor Currie	15 0 0
Doctor M'Keller	10 0 0
Doctor M'Nicoll	10 0 0
McEwin, Midwife, Kildalton	5 0 0

N.B. The allowance of Ten pounds to William Campbell, Surgeon, to be separately stented upon the Twenty pound land of Oa, and the other Medical assessments to be laid upon the Remaining part of the Island."

"The Meeting require that the Medical gentlemen who receive annual allowances from this Meeting do produce a distinct list of all the poor Patients they have attended during the course of the Year, and the medicines bestowed upon such Patients."

1835 "It was ... unanimously approved of, that instead of levying the Cess and Contingencies on the Estate of Islay by the extent of land as has been the practice in time past; the same shall be charged as a percentage upon the whole Rental of Islay. . . ."

1836 It was moved that the dinner which had been assessed on the public be discontinued and was carried on the casting vote of the Chairman.

1837 "It was proposed ... that Malcolm McNeill, Esquire, Lossit, be requested to correspond with his friends in Edinburgh to ascertain the best mode of getting a Post office established in Port Ellin. . . . ."

1838 "A Motion was made, seconded, and carried, that the Receiving houses and Post Runners hitherto paid out of the General Meeting Assessment should in future be discontinued."

Acts of the Bailliary of Islay. 1715 An Act against Brybrie. 1721 against giving anything to "Thiggers or Sorners." 1725 against stealing horses or cattle; transporting servants or any other persons to other countries, especially to Ireland; weavers to "take the meall of the Country at the rate of the Country for their Work"; that "shoemakers work the common whang at a shill. Scots per every single pair . . . that taylors work at four shill. Scots per day . . . that all servants that shall be found to be fourty days out of service after they Leave their former Masters and not engaged with ane oyr. master shall pay ten merks Scots of fine, and that every woman that shall be found out of service as above to pay five merks Scots of fine, . . ." 1729. Standing Rules and Statutes in this Island. Which include "That any servant who lives over year in the Country till harvest, And shall then remove to any other place out of the Island, And after harvest time returns again Shall upon his return be put in Stocks for four days & nights. . . ."

Here the book ends.

It is not at all clear when the money stented for the repair of the bridges and the enclosing of the churchyards was paid and the work completed. A great deal of time was spent talking about the paquet and about the postal service.

The Ellister Murders of 1698

JOHN McVEIR alias MacDonald of Elistererrarich in Islay was arrested on 22 May 1699 and brought before the Baillie of Islay, Archibald Campbell of Cluaness, and on 8th. June appeared before Mr John Campbell, brother of the Earl of Argyll, Justice Depute of Argyllshire, and confessed to murder and four separate thefts of sheep and goats in Islay and elsewhere, on each occasion. In view of the grave nature of the crime he appeared in Inveraray before Mr John Campbell and a jury for sentence the next day. The jury of 15 consisted of the Provost, the Baylie, three merchants, a surgeon, a carpenter, a gardener, a smith, a wright, a saddler, a maltman and three other men.

He was accused of the crime of murder and manslaughter which is reputed odious and atrocious, severely punishable with loss of life and confiscation of the movable property of the committer thereof, that he did upon a day in the previous September unknown with force and violence cast and throw one CHRISTIAN McMILLAN the wife of DONALD McKENZIE in Ellister over a rock at Ellister shore, where they had gone to collect shellfish, into the deep sea where she was immediately drowned and died. The alleged motive which John did not dispute was that he committed this crime to conceal another crime being the murder of MOIR McILCHENICH widow in Ellister and we are told that the last mentioned murder of the widow was "discovered" (probably means committed) by him and others. Which would seem to imply that he murdered Christian to prevent her telling about the murder of the widow. In view of the confessions made the jury were satisfied and formally pronounced John guilty. The Dempster was called into court by the ringing of a bell and recited the sentence as recorded by the Clerk of the Court adding "This I give for doom." Therefore the said Justice Depute by the mouth of Duncan McIlvory Dempster of Court adjudged and ordained the above named to be taken upon the twelfth day of this instant month of June being Monday next to the ordinary place of execution and then and there be hanged upon a Gibbet till he die the death and his right hand to cut off and to be affixed to the most conspicuous place of the tollbooth of Killvorow in Ila there to continue till it rot or wear away, and ordained his moveables to be confiscated.

DONALD McKENZIE of Ellister, EFFERICK McKENZIE, wife of John McVeir alias McDONALD and sister of DONALD McKENZIE, and KATHARIN NcINDUGHLASSIE of Ellister were arrested and brought before Archibald Campbell of Cluaness Baillie of Islay on 16 May 1699 (a full year after the crime is said to have been committed and six days before John McVeir was taken before the Baillie). Katharin McMILLAN wife of DUNCAN McKENZIE should have been with them but by that time was dead. They were charged that they did contrive, design and plot to murder MOIR NcILCHENICH widow of Ellister for mere avarice and covetousness to attain to her money which they supposed she had lying by her in her house and in pursuance of this plot did upon some day of April 1698 in dead time of night murder her by strangling her with her own belt and thereafter threw her body over a rock into the sea so that the deed was not discovered for some time. They confessed to plotting and executing the murder. On the 8th June 1699, the same day as the trial of John McVeir, they appeared before the Justice Depute at Inveraray and adhered to the confession made in Islay. The jury were satisfied and they were sentenced to hanging.

It looks as though John McVeir was a party to Moir McIlchenich's murder although he was never charged with it, and we can only speculate as to what the three accused said before the Baillie on 16th May which induced the authorities to apprehend John McVeir and bring him before the Baillie on 22nd May 1699 — did they "split" on him?

Clearances

A QUESTION which is often asked is, are the large number of derelict buildings on the island the result of clearances? The answer is undoubtedly — Yes, in most cases, but the enquirer may possibly be disappointed to hear that there was no burning of houses and no use of soldiers in red coats. They were peaceable, but none the less enforced clearances. We are not concerned here with the morality of such actions but there is no doubt that most of the people evicted did not want to leave their home, a home that they or their forebears had built with their own hands and enlarged as the family increased. They were primitive by modern standards and life, just to exist, was a very hard one, but they were home and many of those who lived in these remote parts had probably never been further away than the nearest celebration of Holy Communion. Whatever the method the reason was the same, the amalgamation of a lot of small holdings into sheep farms, and the result a very different pattern of agriculture. Plots of land were provided where houses could be built near the coast and it was hoped that fishing would become the occupation of former crofters; it was the beginning of the villages. It is known that many families emigrated to Canada during the fifty years from 1818 to 1868 and a great number of them came from the crofts.

The true story emerges from the evidence given to the Royal Commission (Highlands & Islands) 1892, and from many questions asked, a few answers are taken as illustration. In answer to one question, Duncan MacIndeor, a 75 years old roadman from Kilmeny said, "I was a farmer at Airidh-Ghuairidh for 23 years. There were many others as well as myself put out or deprived of their parks about this time to make room for Webster [the under factor for whom the house at Daill Farm was built]. Four tenants got notice to leave Airidh-Ghuairidh; six or seven got notice to leave Strongaig. At or about that time Rostern contained four who had to be moved from their holdings. Nosebridge had eight tenants who were also moved; Conegarry also contained eight tenants; Benveridle also contained seven tenants, and four farmers got notice to quit Kilbranan and three to quit Dranich; in other words no less than 44 or 45 had to leave their holdings to give scope to Webster and sheep." Donald Orr, millwright of Starchmill, aged 67, named twenty families who went from Killinan, his father being one of them, seven from Kynagarry and three from Courlach, and said some of them went to America. Dugald Ferguson Macfadyen, a merchant at Port Charlotte and Tayvailin, said there were fifteen crofters in Killinallan besides the large farmer, about 40 years ago [1852]. In Gearach seven tenants, in Oalistach eight, in Carn six and at Toronay five.

Gilbert MacArthur a 64 year old fisherman at Port Charlotte said that 63 years ago [1829] the village was built by the people who came from Kilchiaran where there were fourteen families, Lossit thirteen or fourteen and Tormisdale "a good number." Duncan Campbell MacEwan tells of twenty-eight holdings taken from crofters to make the farm at Raineach Mhor.

Peter Reid, the factor on Kildalton Estate (36), in part of his statement said "I don't suppose it is of any consequence to advert to the question of how people were removed, but I don't think we can admit that there were any evictions, and I think there is no need, unless it is wished, to call forward witnesses to show that there were no evictions, at least in the ordinary sense of the word." In answer to one question he said "I might read extracts to show that the great majority of those who left Oa went entirely of their own free will." When he was asked "Do you deny that any of them were forcibly evicted?" he answered "I deny that any were forcibly evicted. The two cases that have been mentioned occurred about ten years afterwards, and these may have been removed against their will. I deny that there were any evictions; they may have got letters of removal, but I deny that these were any evictions in the sense of evictions." "What you mean by eviction is forcible removal?" "Forcible removal. No doubt there would be pressure brought to bear on these two. . . ." "Do you know the former population of Islay and the population at the present day?" "They emigrated. There were about 400 people emigrated in 1863." John Campbell, aged 52, a cottar at Giol, said at one time there were nine tenants there who went to America about 32 years since [1860], there were at least six in Grastle and Tockmal. When asked "Were they forcibly evicted, or did they go of their own free will?" he answered "Some left voluntarily owing to the poor markets." "And were any evicted by force?" to which the answer was "Yes, on the south side of the parish."

Archibald Campbell, a carter in Port Ellen (60), had quite a story to tell. "How did you cease to have land?" "We were forced to stop it." "Where were you at the time?" "In a place called Lurabus first." "How many were in Lurabus besides you?" "Four other crofters besides me." "What became of the others?" "They left." "Do you know where they went to?" "America." He stated that at the time he left, 1859/60, the holdings were made into one large holding. "How long had you a holding there?" "My people were there for generations untold." "Did you leave or were you removed or evicted?" "We left and went to Ballychatrigan." "Why did you leave Ballychatrigan?" "We had to leave to make room for sheep, and go to strange places." "Then when you were removed from Ballychratigan did you go of your own free will?" "We had to go." "Where did you go to?" "Stremnish." "And how long were you there?" "Four years." "Why did you leave Stremnish?" "We were not allowed to stop." "You were again removed from Stremnish?" "Yes." "Why?" "They wanted the land for sheep." "And when you were put out of Stremnish where did you go?" "We came to Port Ellen."

Some boats at Port Ellen pier from 1857

Year	Name	Master	Tons
1857	Arran Maid		
1857-1877	Eclipse	I. Macmillan	40
	Seicena		
1858	Catie & Mary		
	Bethin		
	Nations		
1858-1861	Elizabeth	Holland	32
	John		
	Pearl		
1858-1862	Elizabeth & Mary		45
	Vintage		
1858-1872	Commodore	A. McDougall	36
	Agnes		
	Margaret		
	Oddfellow		
	Curlew		
1858-1865	Jeans & Mary	Finlay Smith	36
1858-1860	Caledonia		
	Mary Anne		
1858-1860	Caledonia		
	Mary Anne		
1858-1865	Oracle	McLauchlin	44
1858-1871	St. George	Capt. Munchy	
1858 & 1860	Helen		
	Walter Frederick		
1859	Charlotte		
	James	McKim in 1865	37
	Cochrin Henry		
	James Irving		
	Inveraray Castle		
	Princess		
	Stork		
	Clansman		
1859, 62, 68	Jean & Helen	Capt. MacMillan	37
	Manthidiov Ree		
1859 & 1860	Friends		
	Charming Peggie		

Year	Name	Master	Tons
1859-1873	Islay Schooner	Capt. Burns	43
	Pilot		
	Margaret McGeown		
	Catherine		
	Ellen		
	Sark		
	Rose	Mathison in 1866	25
1860	Jean		
	Agnes & Mary		
	Mary Jean		
	Georgina		
	Greenock steamer		
1861	Unicorn	McLachlan	58
1861	Sir Charles Napier	D. McDougall	13
	Alloa	Jas. Crawford	50
	Fire Fly	John Barbour	6
	Flower	Croll	31
	Dove	McCallum	55
1862	Albion	Douglas	160
	St. Kilda	Capt. Colquhon	91
	Bee	Peter Kelly	35
	Williams	Jas. MacFarlane	34
	Blue Bell	H. Henry	56
	Jeanie Blair	Hunter	59
	Wave	MacCallum	8
	Fingall	Capt. Black	8
1862	Brothers	Thomas Manie	59
	Kitty	Capt. McKay	8
	Brothers		34
	Elizabeth	Capt. Vaughan	28
	Wallace	Capt. Gray	42
1862 & 1864	Express	Capt. Wilson	57
	Advance	Capt. Birrell	45
1863	Lady of the Lake	Doven	28
1863-1874	Christina	D. McMillan	32
1863-1868	Jane & Ellen	McMillan	37
	Lark	McIntyre	50
	Eliza	McKay	56

Year	Name	Master	Tons
1864	Malnit	Baxter	53
	Isabella Clark	Sillars	25
1865	Fife Packet	Clark	42
1865-1867	Jean & May	Smith	39
	Hadie		55
1866	Glenluce	McPherson	49
1866-1872	Isabella	Kerr	37
1867	Petrel		
	Jorel	Caldwell	147
	Brookspy	Fagan	14
1868 & 1872	Jannet McNab	Leitch	41
1878 & 1870	Eliza	Muschy	50
1869	Brodick	Hamilton	31
	Rose	McDonald	16
	Nancy	McKay	30
1869-1874	Fairy	J. McMillan	49
	Britania	McJames	
	Jura	McPherson	38
	Chiefton	McFarlan	51
1870	Chrystle	Robart?	53
	Mary	D. Blair	42
	Peggy	I. McDonald	38
1873 & 1876	S.S. Celt	McKinnon	63
	Flora Kelso	A. Kelso	53
	Effort	Campbell	35
	Leith	Capt. McKenzie	35
	North Maw	Farlaw	51
	Jannet	Capt. Taylor	36
	Ann McCormick	A. McTavish	49
1871	Coll Castle	N. McKinnon	26
	Broughty Castle	J. McKinnon	66
	Kelpie	Capt. Robertson	49
	Vullutine	Capt. Cochran	54
	Northan	D. McFarlan	51
	Mary Inverness	D. MacDonald	21
1871 & 1872	Elizabeth	John McIntosh	57
	Elizabeth	McCulloch	49
	Argyll	Colghoun	68
	George Brown	Lang	90
	Rescue	Campbell	49
	Jane	McDougall	25
	Margaret	Clark	61
	Marraing Dick	A. Blair	49
	Albart	McCallum	41
1871 & 1875	Dunbarton Castle	Capt. Henderson	41
	Dunvagan Castle	Capt. Smith	149
	Jessie	Capt. King	40
1873	Franch Locker		50
1876 & 1877	Texa	A. McDougall	53
	Victoria	McCay	56
	Arran Maid	McNeill	38
	Banf Packet	McDonald	35
	Rescue	McFederane	56
	Marquess of Lorne	Willie	72
1873 & 1875	Mirtle	Campbell	107
	James & Margaret		48
1873	Mary & Elizabeth	James Taylor	45
	Shamerack	McDorala	25
	Laurel	Melvill	147
	Eringa	McFarlane	67
1875	Anne	Bragiss	32
	Tay	McDougall	36
	Fuan	McCunlay	43
	Isabella	Murchy	45
	Flora	Johnston	37
	Dart	A. McDougall	59
	Martha	Care	30
	Chryoslate	McIntyre	54
1875 & 1876	Naid	C. Brown	44
	Carne	Bussess	32
1875 & 1877	Glasgow	Brown	39
1876	Proceet	D. McQuiene	44
	Tuskar	C. Reaid	250
	Bridalbine		56
	Star	McKinlay	62
	Princess Beatrice	C. Reid	270
1877	Go Ahead	McMillan	58
	Marg. McGown	McMillan	58

More details up to the year 1956 can be found in the Port Ellen Harbour Book which is in the Islay Museum library.

The dues were at the rate of $1\frac{1}{2}$d. a ton, and in some cases a plankage of between one and two shillings.

In March 1861, Donald McDougall writes, — "I hereby acknowledge to have received Fifty five pounds 13/4d sterling being my salary for five years and seven months commencing 15 May 1855 to 15th. December 1860 as Harbour Master at Port Ellen in full during which period I have collected for dues Sixty five pounds 17/$7\frac{1}{2}$ which is now also settled in full."

THE PIER, PORT ELLEN, ISLE OF ISLAY. D.5409

MAIN STREET (LOOKING NORTH), BOWMORE, ISLAY.

Kildalton House, Islay No. 95

White Hart Hotel and Memorial Hall, from Geisgeir Golf Course, Port Ellen, Islay

"Pioneer" at Port Askaig Pier, Islay
43511.

Islay House Gardens. No. 40
43498. J.V.

Photographs by Archibald Cameron, Bowmore, early

Rainfall since 1866

THE annual totals are published with the permission of Islay Estates Ltd. where a remarkably long run of weather statistics has been kept with very few gaps. Yearly totals do not show freak occurrences such as the storm in September 1939. It was a bright sunny morning until about 11.30 a.m. when Prime Minister Chamberlain was just finishing broadcasting that Great Britain was at war with Germany. Then the heavens opened for torrential rain, thunder and lightning and the resulting floods washed away the bridges on the high road from Bridgend to Port Ellen and on the low road over the Machrie river. It was some years before they were replaced and the legend on the present bridge at the airport tells the story; Built 1885. Destroyed in Storm 1939. Rebuilt 1951, but does not say that a Bailey bridge was used during the war.

ANNUAL RAINFALL recorded at EALLABUS, ISLAY.
By courtesy of Islay Estates Ltd.

	ins.		ins.		ins.		ins.		ins.
1866	63.66	1890	52.01	1914	52.75	1937	46.75	1960	50.73
1867	46.91	1891	44.34	1915	40.66	1938	58.64	1961	55.41
1868	55.12	1892	——	1916	51.36	1939	44.84	1962	49.37
1869	47.96	1893	50.08	1917	56.53	1940	54.84	1963	42.20
1870	39.80	1894	46.32	1918	56.52	1941	37.59	1964	50.70
1871	45.52	1895	——	1919	51.82	1942	68.43	1965	49.60
1872	55.68	1896	49.37	1920	58.94	1943	54.63	1966	45.16
1873	44.06	1897	——	1921	52.16	1944	51.71	1967	56.98
1874	50.23	1898	51.80	1922	51.74	1945	46.54	1968	44.37
1875	46.16	1899	48.67	1923	75.82	1946	48.74	1969	47.14
1876	52.01	1900	55.56	1924	57.42	1947	47.97	1970	54.87
1877	64.66	1901	46.79	1925	56.21	1948	60.91	1971	37.75
1878	45.12	1902	43.65	1926	64.10	1949	54.33	1972	48.89
1879	44.80	1903	58.00	1927	53.43	1950	60.67	1973	48.85
1880	39.48	1904	51.73	1928	72.06	1951	49.65	1974	51.20
1881	46.40	1905	51.79	1929	61.55	1952	46.96	1975	46.71
1882	55.99	1906	50.12	1930	65.11	1953	51.75	1976	50.16
1883	56.27	1907	55.80	1931	52.99	1954	67.06	1977	51.23
1884	54.11	1908	51.22	1932	50.34	1955	44.06	1978	48.58
1885	46.47	1909	47.90	1933	39.46	1956	45.94	1979	54.91
1886	49.01	1910	48.29	1934	48.20	1957	46.99	1980	56.69
1887	38.78	1911	49.89	1935	42.26	1958	42.33	1981	53.49
1888	45.76	1912	53.99	1936	46.99	1959	47.50	1982	54.90
1889	44.17	1913	47.02						

Range: highest 75.82 in 1923
Range: lowest 37.59 in 1941

25 years average
1886-1890 49.20 ins.
1891-1915 47.52
1916-1940 54.80
1941-1965 50.87
1966-1980 49.56
(15 years)

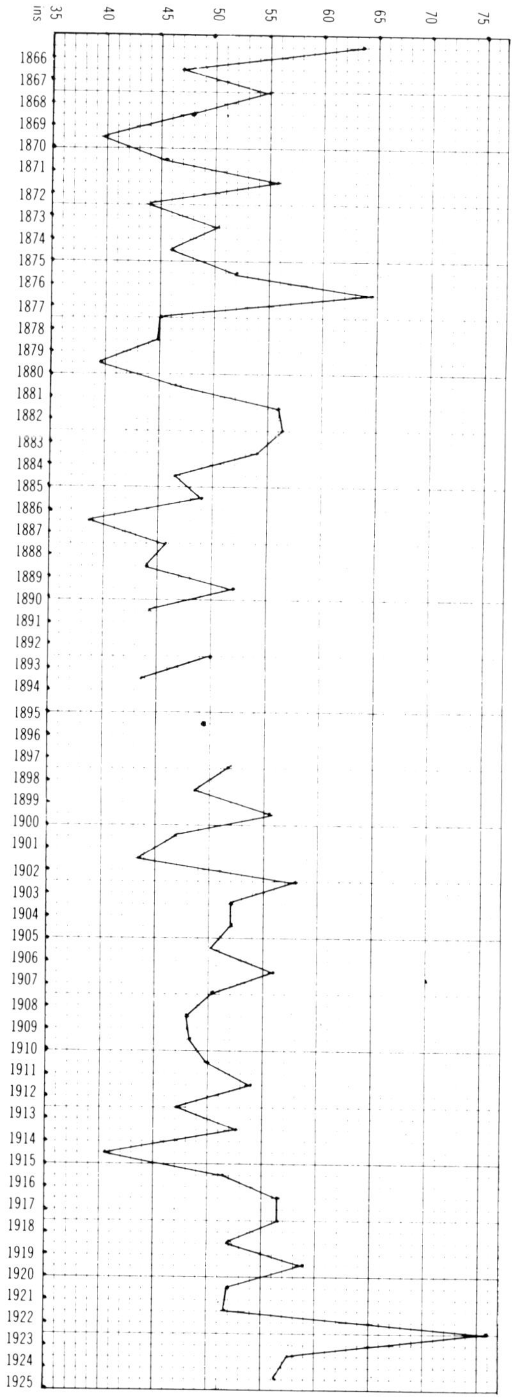
ins
35
40
45
50
55
60
65
70
75
1866
1867
1868
1869
1870
1871
1872
1873
1874
1875
1876
1877
1878
1879
1880
1881
1882
1883
1884
1885
1886
1887
1888
1889
1890
1891
1892
1893
1894
1895
1896
1897
1898
1899
1900
1901
1902
1903
1904
1905
1906
1907
1908
1909
1910
1911
1912
1913
1914
1915
1916
1917
1918
1919
1920
1921
1922
1923
1924
1925

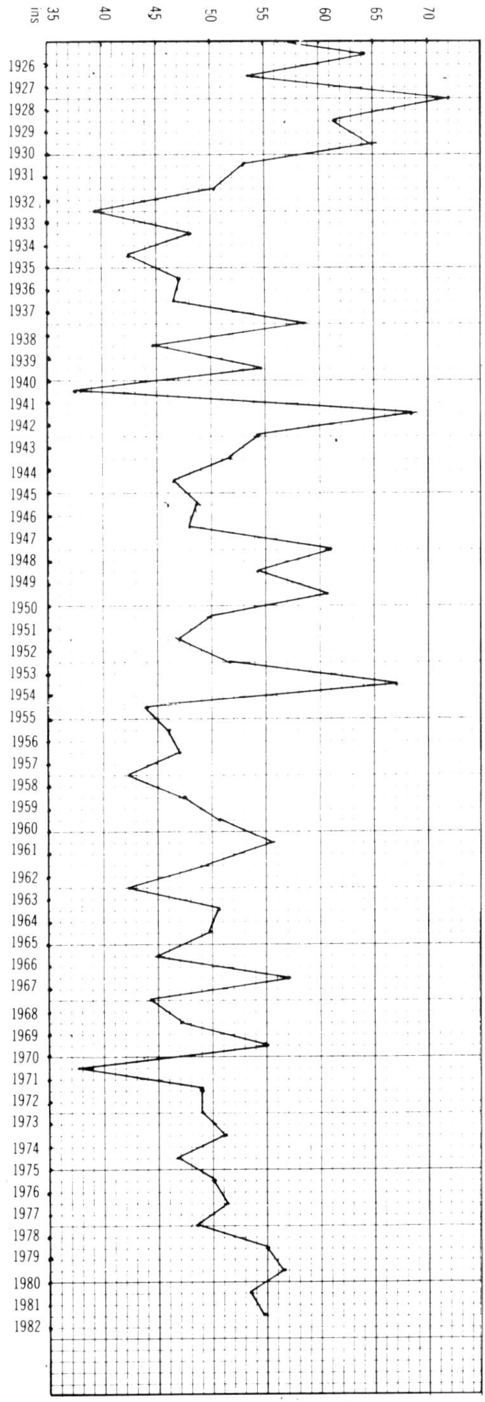
ins
35
40
45
50
55
60
65
70
1926
1927
1928
1929
1930
1931
1932
1933
1934
1935
1936
1937
1938
1939
1940
1941
1942
1943
1944
1945
1946
1947
1948
1949
1950
1951
1952
1953
1954
1955
1956
1957
1958
1959
1960
1961
1962
1963
1964
1965
1966
1967
1968
1969
1970
1971
1972
1973
1974
1975
1976
1977
1978
1979
1980
1981
1982

Falconry

CAPTAIN Gilbert Blaine was living at Cairnmore, Port Ellen, when he published his book "Falconry," number XV in the Sportsman's Library, in 1936. He kept different types of hawks on blocks in the garden and used the stables as mews. He hunted, mostly with peregrines, on the Cairnmore estate, including the Oa, Ballivicar, Glenmachrie, Leorin and Kilbride, and would appear to have had considerable success.

	Grouse	Blackgame	Partridge	Pheasant	Woodcock	Snipe	Duck	Hare	Various
1933	54	3	3	2				2	
1934	96	2	1	17	2				2
1935	99	4	1	15	3				
1936	178	4	6	8	7				
1937	129		1		1	1	1		1

There are no records after these but he was still on the island shooting and during the war commanded the Islay Home Guard. In 1936 he wrote "Nowadays the trouble and expense involved in keeping a stud of hawks is so great that only a fortunate few are able to do so."

"Let it not be imagined that grouse are an easy quarry for any hawk to take. Only the best and fastest falcons can kill them regularly after September, and very few tiercels." (male peregrine)

"Young blackgame are easily taken by falcons, but an old blackcock can take care of himself."

George E. Lodge whose excellent paintings have illustrated so many bird books, visited Gilbert Blaine at Cairnmore during September and October of the mid-1930s on three occasions. In his book "Memoirs of an Artist Naturalist" (1954) he mentions these visits, quoting from his diary for "September 24, 1936, hawking in the afternoon with a gyr-falcon which the late Ernest Vesey (pen name of Ernest Lewis) had brought back from Iceland." Actually it was one of six eyases according to Stanley Cerely in "The Gyr-Falcon Adventure" 1935. This bird was flown at blackcock but grey hens and hen pheasants were too easy for him and eventually, after killing a grouse about a mile away, he disappeared and was not seen again. George Lodge and Gilbert Blaine must have been old acquaintances for they were hawking together in Caithness in 1913. In Islay in September 1938 they were flying a peregrine falcon at grouse with a bird called Cressida. He says that Blaine's falconer in Islay was Leonard Potter.

Any falconer hunting these grounds nowadays would be fortunate to get a handful of grouse in a season and there are no partridges.

Libraries

THE eminent novelist and philosopher Iris Murdoch was asked in an interview in 1982 "What do you think of other forms and media, such as television?" and I could not agree more with her reply which was "People say that British television is the best in the world but there is so much violence and such a lot of it is so terrible. Television has altered people's lives immensely — I feel very hostile to it. Much of it is awful and yet so technically good. I see television as a sort of crime against the world. There is such a tremendous difference between terribly good television pictures and the real world; people become addicted to looking at it instead of what's about them. It's very important that young people should read books they don't want to read; it would be a great pity if they didn't read the literature of the past."

Lord Bannerman wrote "The Highlander's greatest asset is his insatiable desire for education."

When crossing by boat from West Loch Tarbert to Port Ellen on one of my early journeys to Islay I was talking with an elderly minister who was coming to visit a crofter brother who was ill, and during our conversation I said that it appeared to me that for a small island with a population of about four thousand it had produced an unusually large proportion of ministers, ship captains, marine engineers and doctors and asked him why he thought that was so. He replied that it was because in his youth there was little to do in their spare time except read and study. One can imagine their need of concentration with the family trying to keep warm round a peat fire in a dark room, reading by the light of a flickering homemade candle or smoky paraffin lamp but perhaps it was easier than trying to compete with a noisy television set a century later. I suspect that they also had scholarly and dedicated teachers and well read ministers and the encouragement of parents who realised that the only chance their children had of improving their way of life was by having the best education possible which would enable them to compete for the limited number of places which were available in the colleges and universities. Many of those who became tradesmen and stayed on the island had a remarkable range of knowledge, an interest in the history of their island and its legends, knew a great deal of the Gaelic poetry of the bards and the native songs, could quote extensively from the Bible and Gaelic proverbs and often had an unusually accurate memory of dates. One occasionally comes across a man who is almost a recluse and one wonders how he manages to make a living for he doesn't seem very interested in doing so. It takes time and patience to get these quiet slow spoken people to talk; they must be sure that one is not trying to make a fool of them or mocking them. But if one manages to gain their confidence the reward is a feast of learning and interesting comment which can only have been acquired by a lifetime spent largely in reading. One is left wondering whether it was a dream or one really had been listening to a man whose clothes and surroundings were obviously of little importance but who knew more Latin and Greek than one ever had, could quote the classics and poetry, would have one lost in the depths of philosophy, someone who was probably in a Gaelic world of his own and was translating into English for the benefit of his listener although the learning had largely been gathered in that language.

In a community like this the printed word has always been of more importance than to most of those whose access to books was very much easier. Sometimes the laird or the minister recognised this need and a literary society was formed. Andrew Carnegie was one of those enlightened people who provided libraries for rural areas on the mainland and certainly not the only one; sometimes people got together under the leadership of the minister or the doctor and formed their own society. The earliest evidence there is in Islay was the Port Ellen News & Reading Room which was opened in 1858 but there is no clue in the minutes as to where it was. The minute for the first of April begins "In the spring of the present year a few friends convened themselves together for the purpose of considering the possibility of opening a News & Reading Room." What strikes one about the names of the "few friends" is that there are so few of what one might call Islay family names. John Hart Estcourt, George and John Ross, James Mackerrell, James Scott, Edward Skinner, Duncan McKenzie, Duncan McArthur, John Gilchrist, Duncan and Peter McDougall, William Morris, James Kennedy, John Kenyon and William Glass. In addition James Stein was appointed a vice-president and John McDonald, Alex McTaggart and Dr. Crawford added to the membership. John Ramsay provided a room and also supplied regularly "The North British Daily Mail." James Scott gave "The Illustrated London News," "Chamber's Journal" and "Leisure Hour" and the members purchased "The London Daily Times" (at half price), "Edinburgh Witness," "Glasgow Saturday Post," "Edinburgh Weekly Mercury," "Punch," "National Magazine" and "Christian Treasury." The subscription was 5/- a year if paid in one sum or 1/6 a quarter but all persons under 20 years of age one shilling quarterly, for which they received a signed ticket of admission and also had the privilege of introducing a lady to the free lectures, the members themselves were admitted (at half price) to lectures where a charge was made. Strangers were allowed in the news room on payment of one penny put into the Strangers Box. The room was open from 8 a.m. to 10 p.m. on Monday, Wednesday, Thursday and Saturday and 6 a.m. to 11 p.m. on Tuesday and Friday. The papers were sold off quarterly; "Punch" at 1½d a copy and "The London Times" at 5/3 a quarter. Soon "The Glasgow Examiner," "The Londonderry Standard" and "West of Scotland Review" were taken and "The Glasgow Saturday Post" dropped. It was agreeed that "The Times" could be taken out of the room from 10 p.m. to 8 a.m. next morning.

The official inaugural meeting did not take place until October when the room had been open six months, and took the form of a Tea Soirée. The Port Ellen Sacred Harmony Class sang a few anthems and Miss Shaw played the piano. Addresses were given by Rev. Alexander McKenzie of

Port Ellen, who spoke on "Mental Culture," John G. Lerach of Lagavulin on "Education," Hector McLean of Ballygrant on "Agriculture" and John Hart Estcourt on "Ways and Means." Mr John Ramsay presided.

By the end of the first year the members felt sufficiently established to start collecting books and money for the library and had been asked to send a copy of their rules to Oban where it was hoped to form a similar society. A resolution was passed that "nothing relating to Total Abstinence be introduced into the News and Reading room lectures.

On the formation of a library it was resolved "that this library in conjunction with the News Room is instituted to form one Institution to be called the Port Ellen Mechanics Institution." Its prosperity depended on the enthusiasm of one or two people as so many other island institutions have always done and some periods were much more active than others. After 1860 the monthly meetings became almost formal and were often postponed, the records were inadequate and subscriptions so far behind that they were cancelled. Then the meetings became little more than quarterly distributions of the papers. There was a revival in 1865 with a stocktaking and a new set of rules, which amongst other alterations allowed ladies to become members by subscribing 6d a quarter. A gradual decline is evident until the records cease in November 1872 although the last entry was "to take immediate steps to prepare for the Soirée." There are several blank pages after this but perhaps another minute book, now lost, was started. During the latter years the only minute of interest was in October 1869 when "the secretary was empowered to write to Mr Menzies and Dr. Campbell, the former from taking any papers and the latter from entering the room altogether, not being a subscriber." In 1870 there was a complaint about the pilfering of papers and the committee have to acknowledge, with regret, that their attempts to prevent this evil have not been attended with such success as had been anticipated." In the autumn of 1870 "a Diamond Lamp with oil" was purchased and it was "to be kept burning for the first two nights after the receipt of papers and Mr John Slater was granted "the use of the Reading Room for one night in the week to have exercises in music."

The publications taken were constantly changing and it would appear that "Punch" was the only one which was taken throughout the whole period. The papers included: Glasgow Herald, Scotsman, North British Daily Mail, News of the World, London Daily Telegraph, Daily Herald, Glasgow Morning Journal, Argyllshire Herald, Glasgow Saturday Post, Inverness Courier, Temperance Weekly Journal, Saturday Post, Weekly Northern Whig, Greenock Herald, Weekly Scotsman, Oban Times, Glasgow Weekly Mail, Scottish Review, Belfast Weekly News, Coleraine Chronicle in 1870; the magazines included: Macmillan's, Frazer's, Blackwood's, Chamber's Encyclopedia, The Builder, Agricultural Journal, Practical Mechanic's Journal, North British Agriculturalist; also The Band of Hope Review, Bulwark, Reformer's Gazette, The British Workman, Family Treasury, Leisure Hour, Christian Treasury, Good Words, The Highland Society's Journal, London Society, New York Journal of Commerce. In

1860 £2-10-0 was voted for the purchase of Gaelic books; the catalogue of 1865 contained 25 titles.

This was out of 329 volumes which were left after 150 titles were reported missing at the time of the 1865 review. Of these there were 57 volumes under the heading *Religious & Moral,* including works by Doddridge, Bunyan, Calvin, Knox, Dick, Beecher, Butler and D'Aubigne; 19 volumes *Scientific* with books on Natural Philosophy, Geology, Astronomy, Agricultural Chemistry, Phrenology, The Art of Cooking and an Ornithological Guide to Shetland. Only 9 books of *Travels;* 36 of Biography ten of them being Boswell's Samuel Johnson, also Macaulay's "Clive" and "Warren Hastings," Taylor's "Sir Robert Peel," Irving's "Christopher Columbus." 21 books of *Poetry* and 50 of *History* with Rollin's "Ancient History" in twelve volumes and Rapin's "History of England" in fifteen; but only two on the "History of Scotland" by Buchanan, two of Walker's "History of the Hebrides," Gregory's "Western Highlands" and Clelland's "Rise and Progress of Glasgow." Amongst the *Miscellaneous* "The Compleat Angler" by Walton, five volumes of "Humbolt's Cosmos," eight of Burk's "Works" and "Speeches," "Robinson Crusoe" by Defoe, and "Uncle Tom's Cabin" by Stowe.

The titles of the lectures included: Dr. Crawford on "The four stages of man's existence considered in relation to Health and disease" and later on "Physiology;" Mr Hector McLean on "Taste," "Highland Poetry & Romance" and "The Study of Geology;" Mr Chisholm on "Social Reform;" Mr Lerach on "Burns;" Mr Dewar on "Electricity;" Mr Coath on "The Acquisition of Knowledge," "The Study of Political & Constitutional History and its bearing on Christianity" and "Mental Philosophy;" Rev. Hugh Monroe on "The Connection of Revelation with Geology" and "Our English Bible;" Rev. McFadyen on "Rising in Life;" Dr. Blair on "The Atmosphere" and "Health" where he condemned the Port Ellen water supply; Colin Hay on "Agriculture & Commerce" and "Instinct & Reason."

The programmes of two Soirées are worth recording; the one in October 1865 started with a Public Tea at 6 o'clock precisely and was followed by the

	Chairman's Address	
Duet	Tis the hour for music	Mrs Baker & Miss Russell
Song	Scenes of Home	Mr Bate
	Address — Rev. J. McFadyen	
Song	Auld Robin Gray	Miss Russell
Duet	What are the Wild Waves Saying	Mr Bate & Mrs Baker
	Address — Capt. J. C. Graham	
Song	Paddle your own Canoe	Mr Baker
Song	Nightingale's Trill	Mrs Baker
Song	My Hieland Hame	Mr H. May
	Address — Mr H. McLean Gaelic	

Song	Gaelic	Mr Sinclair
	15 minute interval for a service of fruit	
Song	Oh for the bloom of my own native Heather	Miss Russell
Duet	Tobacco Controversy	Mr & Mrs Baker
	Address — Mr Angus McCuaig	
Song	Clean your boots	Mr Bate
Song	Barney O'Hea	Mr Baker
	Vote of thanks to the Ladies; to the speakers & singers	
Song & Chorus	God Bless the Prince of Wales	Mr Baker & company
	Vote of thanks to the Chairman	
Anthem	God Save the Queen	Mrs Baker & company
Song	Auld Lang Syne	Miss Russell & company

306 tickets were sold, the cost was £16-19-9 and made a profit of £4. Amongst other things they consumed 10 lbs of tea, 150 apples, 174 lbs currant cakes, 356 buns, 220 Perkins, 12 lbs butter and three gallons of cream.

At a stocktaking in October 1869 they had 421 cups, 521 saucers, 104 plates and 127 yards of white cotton.

The Soirée on 23rd December 1869 took place in one of the distillery lofts "a few minutes after six o'clock when the hall was completely crowded, upwards of 600 persons being present." After the Soirée an Assembly took place, dancing commenced about ten o'clock and was kept up with great spirit until about twelve o'clock when all departed peaceably to their homes. They started with a Blessing then Tea followed by the chairman's remarks.

Anthem	The Earth is the Lord's	Choir
Song	Bonnie Scotland I adore thee	Mr Fairbairn
Song	Gaelic	Mr Donald McArthur
	Address in Gaelic	Mr Hector McLean
Song	The Boattie Rows	Choir
Duet	The Minute Gun at sea	Messrs Glass & Fairbairn
Song	Comic	Mr Fairbairn
	Service of fruit	
Address	Tour in Egypt	Mr John Ramsay
Song	Germany	Miss Nora Campbell
Song	The Banks of Doon	Choir
Song	Gaelic	Mr Angus McCuaig
Song	Nil Desperandum	Mr Fairbairn
Song	Comic	Mr Donald Campbell
	Votes of thanks	
Anthem	God Save the Queen	Choir

The accounts also show 5/- paid to a piper.

By this date there must have been a very fine library at Islay House collected over the two hundred years since it was built; one cannot imagine that Eallabus which produced Dr. John Crawford who wrote "A History of the Indian Archipelago" and "A Grammar & Dictionary of the Malay Language," and the distinguished surgeon Professor Cheine, was without a library. Hector McLean the eminent scholar in Anthropology and Celtic Literature who gave so much help to J. F. Campbell in the preparation of "Popular Tales of the West Highlands" must have had a good library and another schoolmaster at Ballygrant, Neil MacAlpine, cannot have compiled his Gaelic Dictionary without one. John Ramsay had a useful library at Kildalton and the sight in recent years of the doors of his beautiful built-in book cases with broken glass and flapping in the wind could almost make one weep. These and possibly smaller collections held by some ministers would rarely be available.

The most interesting library and the most difficult to understand is the ROBERT BLAIR MEMORIAL library in Portnahaven. Most of this collection, which is now of about one thousand volumes, was purchased from the Reverend Dr. Blair's widow by the Rhinns Hall committee in 1933. The main interest is in the wide range of the books and the difficulty in knowing which were Dr. Blair's books and which have been added.

Although Robert Blair was born at Bullwood, Dunoon, on 3rd May 1837, he had strong Islay connections. A William Blair died at Gortontoid in 1850. Robert's father, Duncan, died at Bowmore in 1867, aged 85; his mother, Margaret Campbell in 1874. The family lived at Lonbàn near Corrary, as is evident from William Livingston's dedication in his poem Fios thun a'bhaird. He was educated at Bowmore school and Glasgow University where he obtained his M.A. in 1863 and was made a Doctor of Divinity in 1891. As a Gaelic scholar his greatest work was the collation and editing of William Livingston's poems, with his own memoir and introduc-

Ballinaly House destroyed by fire in 1933.

tory criticism, and was one of the translators of the Revised version of the Bible into Gaelic. He died in Edinburgh in 1907.

In 1934 the Hall Committee made a set of regulations for lending which were stuck in each book on a numbered bookplate; the highest number remaining is over 800. Members paid a fee of one shilling a year and one penny a week for each book borrowed. The librarian attended from 7 p.m. to 8 p.m. on Thursday evenings.

Difficulties arise because there does not seem to have been any system of numbering or any attempt to group subjects. For example, the three volumes of Boswell's "Life of Johnson" are numbered 228, 239 and 241. There are a number of works of which there is more than one copy, which would seem to indicate that other collections were added to Dr. Blair's before the numbering was done. There are many volumes un-numbered and many which were numbered seem to have been lost or given away. Although it would have been interesting to have known which were Dr. Blair's books and where the others came from, the important point is to realise what a very wide range of reading was available to the small number of people in this village. A large proportion of the books were most probably unread.

One would expect works on Religion, Philosophy and the English Classics in the library of a scholar but it is surprising to find that there are only a handful of books in Gaelic in the collection of one of the translaters of the Holy Scriptures into that language. Perhaps such volumes are amongst those lost.

Lists of books can be tedious but such a selection from various subjects is necessary to provide a proper picture of this collection. There are J. Butler "The Anthology of Religion," Max Muller "Life and Religion" and "Physical Religion," Pascal "Thoughts on Religion," Thomas à Kempis "The Imitation of Christ." For the psychologist Mellone & Drummond "Elements of Psychology," W. J. Dauson "The Autobiography of a Mind," John Locke "On the Human Understanding," Paul Dubois "The Influence of the Mind on the Body," Maurice "Moral and Metaphysical Philosophy," Henry Cary "The Dialogues of Plato," John Gillies "Aristotle's Ethics" and W. Jennings "The Confucian Analects." Amongst the political works are David Hume "Essays Literary, Moral and Political," "Selections from Speeches and Writings" of Edmund Burke, John Stuart Mill "The Principles of Political Economy" and later, Philip Snowden "Socialism Syndicalism," and Sidney Webb "Socialism and Individualism."

There are ten volumes of Ruskin, "The Education Library" by Amos Comenius who was the first to illustrate childrens' books, "English Prose Style" by Herbert Read and J. S. Fletcher "Bowmont and Fletcher."

There is not a great deal of poetry but a very varied selection. Sir Walter Scott, John Dryden, Longfellow, John Milton, Burns, Lord Lytton "Odes and Epodes of Horace," C. J. Power "Junior School Poetry" and poems by Stephen Phillips, H. H. Alex Machie and Mamie Richardson.

There are some well bound sets of such works as Sir Walter Scott, and some of the English classics like Charles Dickens, and also the well-known works of Shakespeare, Addison, Tobias Smollett, Chaucer, W. M. Thackray, Charles Kingsley, Oliver Goldsmith, Charlotte Brontë, Mrs Gaskell, Jane Austen and George Eliot with Voltaire, Victor Hugo, Alexander Dumas and Cervantes.

Amongst biography are H. E. Marshall "The Story of Oliver Cromwell" and F. E. Sellar of "Lord Roberts," Boswell "Life of Johnson," John Morley "Life of Gladstone," Pierre de Lano "The Empress Eugenie," May Wynne "Henry of Navarre," Sir Alfred Lyall "Warren Hastings" and H. Firth "The Earl of Shaftsbury."

Travel is not well represented and the books are general; "Imperial Guide to India," "Wonders of the World," Peacock on "Canada," Sir C. Wilson "Picturesque Palestine" and F. Gregson "Letters from Ceylon." "Wildlife in Australia" by W. H. Sonef could be travel or natural history of which there is very little; J. D. Hooker "Botany," M. E. Cooke "Manual of Botany" and J. F. Gemmill "Natural History in the Poetry of Burns," and perhaps, William Durham on "Astronomy" might be included.

Amongst a few health books are J. McGregor-Robertson "The Household Physician," Professor Kirk "Papers on Health," Lyster "First Hygiene" and F. Phillips "Out of Darkness into Light."

Manuals include two on navigation, William Borham "The Theory and Practice of Navigation" and John Don "Navigation." There are also W. S. Bruce "Mountain Climbing," J. Moray Brown "Polo," W. Pole "The Theory of Whist," Horace Hutchinson "Hints on Golf," William Wells "Book of Reference for Farmers" and M. F. Sayers "Household Arithmetic."

As one might expect there are representative works by A. Conan Doyle, R. L. Stevenson, J. Galsworthy, Arnold Bennet, R. M. Ballantyne "Ungava," Harriet Beecher Stowe "Uncle Tom's Cabin," H. G. Wells, Joseph Conrad "Typhoon," and Rider Haggard "She."

The wide range of novels typical of the first third of the twentieth century is perhaps unexpected and almost all the best sellers are there. G. A. Henty, Stanley Weyman, Baroness van Hutten "Pam at Fifty," G. K. Chesterton, P. G. Wodehouse, William Le Queux, E. Phillips Oppenheim, Ian Hay, Beverley Nichols, George Borrow, "Taffrail," P. C. Wren "Beau Geste," Joseph Hocking, A. C. Benson, Raphael Sabatini, Anthony Trollope, George Merideth, Nat Hawthorne, Neil Munro, E. Temple Thurston, Zane Grey, W. J. Locke, Maude Diver, Gertrude Page, Mrs Humphrey Ward, Ethel M. Dell, Charlotte Younge, Margaret Kennedy, and many others. Someone must have been a "fan" of Rhoda Broughton and contributed eight of her books.

There are always intriguing odd volumes and here are contributions by "An English Governess" who wrote "What I Found Out" and "An Old Girl" with "School Days in France."

A book in the museum library is just labelled Register and on opening is found to be a register of books lent, almost all of them books for children. There were 160 titles and the first borrowings were in the autumn of 1909.

Was this a Coats library? The date is right and amongst the books there was a copy of "Literary Tours" by D. T. Holmes who had so much to do with the establishment of these libraries. It would appear that the small number of pupils in a country school had read all in which they were interested and borrowing declined and it was not until a new set of children were ready for reading that regular lendings became frequent again in 1911 and 1912. Another group used the library in the First World War. In 1932 the library was started again with only 38 volumes, most of which were only out once, in the year when they were first available, and borrowed by only two families. The names of the borrowers indicate that this book must have belonged to the Oa school and the few addresses given were Glenastle, Stremnish and Kinnabus, would seem to confirm this. The first books were taken out mainly by Campbells, Sinclairs and McCuaigs, and Ann and Rose McCuaig must have read almost all of them. There were also McNivens, McLellans and MacCalmans, with the addition of Lamont and Kerr during the war.

The books available were just what one would expect; R. L. Stevenson, Charles Kingsley, Captain Marryat, Fenimore Cooper with more than one title, R. M. Ballantyne at the top with four, Sir Walter Scott with only two. W. M. Thackray was represented by "Pendennis," Mrs Gaskell by "Cranford," Charlotte Bronte by "Jane Eyre," Louisa M. Alcott by "Little Women and Good Wives," Jane Austen by "Northanger Abbey," R. D. Blackmore by "Lorna Doone." The most popular of all was Lewis Carroll's "Alice in Wonderland." Shakespeare was only out twice, and perhaps one can understand why "Ruskin's Selections" and "A Short History of the English People" only once and Herbert Martin's "Selections from the Spectator" not at all, but the "Kipling Reader" would seem to deserve more than one lending. Charles Waterton and Richard Jeffreys were there and Gilbert White's "Natural History of Selborne." Also Maria Edgeworth, Robert Southey, Oliver Goldsmith, Dean Swift, John Bunyan and others. Poetry was popular, e.g. "Palgrave's Golden Treasury" and very popular "The Gaelic Choir" — author not given. There were 36 volumes edited by W. T. Stead which were very much used and included such diverse titles as "Twice one are Two," "Aesop's Fables," "Hymns with Pictures," "The First Birdie Book" and "Nursery Rhymes." The selection is predominantly the English Classics and very little Scottish literature but it is surprising that there were only two Gaelic works; John MacCormick's "Oiteagan O'n Jar" (Breeze from the West) and Rev. A. Clark's "Caraid nan Gaidheal."

Amongst the other volumes "What Katie Did" sounds familiar and one supposes that "The Girls of Marleigh Grange" by M. M. Pollard and "Cicily Among the Birds" by Maude Power were similar, and perhaps "The Mysterious Locket" by Ruth Lym and "The Manse Rose" by Cyril Gray, but what were "The Trotty Book" (Elizabeth Stuart Phelps), "That Loon o' Baxter's" (W. Skinner), and why "Sma' Folk and Bairn Days" (Ingeborg von der Lippekonow) and "Coal-Hunk-Peter and his three wishes" (Wilhelm Hauff)?

The Natural History and Antiquarian Society of Islay had a very few books which were kept in the school at Bowmore but most of them seem to have been lost. What is left of this small library are now in the collection in the Islay Museum. The most important is Robert C. Graham "The Carved Stones of Islay" and others are Frank Adam "Clans, Septs and Regiments of the Scottish Highlands" and two volumes of the "Manual of Map Reading."

The Museum of Islay Life in Port Charlotte has a valuable collection of books and papers. Amongst the important source books are "The Book of Islay," "The Stent Book and Acts of the Baillary of Islay 1718-1843," the three "Statistical Accounts," "The Book of the Thanes of Cawdor" and the two volumes of "Minutes of Evidence" given to the Royal Commission (Highlands & Islands) 1892.

Equally important are a number of Minute Books and Registers including the Port Ellen Harbour Book 1857-1956. Minutes of the Port Ellen News and Reading Room, the Minute Book 1928-1969 of the Islay Branch of the National Farmers' Union, extracts, where there is mention of Islay or Jura, taken from the Minutes of the Presbytery of Kintyre, registers and minute books from a number of Islay churches, school magazines and the complete issue of the community newspaper "Ileach" which was first printed in 1973.

The archaeological section has papers on discoveries reported in the Proceedings of the Society of Antiquaries in Scotland from 1881, reports of more recent excavations and an "Archaeological Gazeteer of Islay" in 1959. The carved crosses and slabs are very well documented in R. C. Graham "The Carved Stones of Islay," W. D. Lamont "Ancient and Mediaeval Sculptured Stones of Islay" and K. A. Steer & J. W. M. Bannerman "Late Mediaeval Sculpture in the West Highlands."

There are a number of volumes in Gaelic and in addition Nigel MacNeill "The Literature of the Highlanders," Professor J. S. Blackie "The Language and Literature of the Scottish Highlands" and Magnus McLean "The Literature of the Highlands." There are, of course, the works of J. F. Campbell (Ian Og Ila) and poems of the local bards, William Livingstone, Thomas Pattison, Duncan Johnston, Nigel MacNeill, Hector McLean.

There are a number of "Guides." Other subjects include Place Names, Folklore, Clan Donald, Natural History with ornithology particularly covered, Geology, Transport, Distilling and a large section under the heading Descriptions. New material is being added all the time and a library list is printed from time to time.

THE BRIDGEND MUTUAL IMPROVEMENT SOCIETY.
1892-1895.

The following extracts from the Minute Book and the Cash Book give a full and proper account of the activities of the society.

The first meeting was held in Newton Public School on the 28th.

December at 8.30 p.m. The Revd. Mr. Stewart was unanimously appointed to take the chair. Mr. Osborne proposed the following Rules for the guidance of the Society, which with some additions were approved of.

Name. Bridgend Mutual Improvement Society.

Composition. Members to be Males or Females and above the age of fifteen admitted on paying One Shilling to Treasurer.

Aims of Society. Shall be to promote a spirit of brotherhood among the Members, stir up a desire for self improvement, smooth and tone down the angularities so largely the product of isolated effort, encourage and stimulate individual endeavour, and in short do everything possible to assist each Member to make the most of his or her God-given talents.

Rules: — Meetings of the Members shall be held every second Thursday at 7.30, unless otherwise fixed by the Society or their Committee, in such a case the Secretary shall intimate to all absent Members the change made. Members absent without satisfactory excuse, shall forfeit a small fine of two pence for each case of absence. The excuse shall be made to the Chairman of the meeting, and by him explained to Members who shall decide whether or not guilty by voting aye or no.

A Chairman shall be appointed for each meeting, at the close of which he shall name the Chairman for the one following, and the Member so named shall act in that capacity, unless the Meeting by a majority agree to some other.

At each Meeting of the Society a subject of debate shall be fixed on, and two members appointed to read papers one for the affirmative the other the negative, twenty minutes being allowed for the reading of each paper. The Chairman will then call the names of Members in order of list, when each individual will require to express his or her opinion on the subject. A vote will then be taken when each Member will vote for affirmative or negative, if there still be time, the Chairman will call on Members in order of list when each shall be compelled to contribute a song, Reading or Recitation or in default forfeit threepence for the good of the Society.

Each Member shall feel himself or herself in honour bound as a private individual to abstain from hostile or hurtful criticism, either of the doings of the Society or the individual Members of the same.

The Secretary shall minute the proceedings of each meeting such minutes to be produced, and read and passed at each sederunt.

Any Member feeling himself or herself aggrieved in any way in connection with the Society, shall bring his or her complaint to the Secretary, who will bring it before first meeting.

The Treasurer shall draw up an annual Report which shall be audited and submitted to the Society.

It was proposed by Mr. James Cowan and unanimously agreed that Hector Macfadyen be appointed Secretary and Treasurer.

The following Committee were appointed, viz. Misses Stirling and McGregor and Messrs Osborne, Christie, Borland, McKay, Brown and

Macfadyen, the latter to act as Convener.

The foregoing Committee shall have full power to arrange for the nights and subjects, and also to fix the nights for Magic Lantern Entertainments. Following which nineteen members were elected.

The next meeting was held on 11th. January 1894, when twenty members were present. "The subject of Debate 'Should women be allowed to appear in a public capacity' was discussed, Mr. Osborne leading on the affirmative side, and Mr. James Christie on the negative. The discussion then became general after which both leaders replied, the vote was taken when eleven voted for negative and eight for affirmative. It was moved and unanimously agreed that all private Members be allowed five minutes in the general discussion, and three minutes afterwards to all who wish it. The leaders in a debate will be allowed to reply. It was further moved and agreed that Members should stand while speaking and address the chair." Five more members were enrolled.

25th. January 1894. "The Chairman after a few remarks called upon Mr. Borland to read his Essay on 'Labour,' after which all the Members in rotation were requested to give their views on the subject. Mr. Alex. Brown then followed with the Gaelic Reading 'Fear-a-choire.' Mr. James Cowan offered to present the Society with fifty parts of Cassells National Library, suggested that the Members would subscribe a sum that would purchase a similar number. . . ." The Revd. Mr. McIver was granted the use of the magic lantern for the exhibition of slides at their Sabbath School Soirèe in Bowmore, provided Messrs. Christie and Macfadyen could attend to work it. There were three new members.

8th. February 1894. "The subject of tonight's debate was to be 'Should the Game of Football be encouraged in the Bridgend District.' Eight voted for the affirmative and negative and the Chairman gave his casting vote in favour." Two new members.

22nd. February 1894. "The Chairman called upon Mr. Hector Macfadyen to read his Essay on 'Heredity' after which the Members in rotation were requested to express their mind on the subject.

Mr. Cowan then laid on the table the fifty volumes from Cassells Library which he presented to the Society."

2nd. March 1894. There was a Magic Lantern Entertainment when Mr. Ferguson's Local Views were exhibited by Messrs. Christie and Macfadyen — obviously using two lanterns. Gaelic Readings were given by Messrs Anderson & McAffer and an English Reading by Mr. McDermid. Gaelic Songs by Messrs. Geo. & Arthur Cowan, C. Dow, Neil McDougall and English Songs by Messrs. James & Alex. Christie & J. Cameron. Collection taken at the door 13/7.

8th. March 1894. "The Chairman after a few opening remarks intimated to the Meeting that the Debate would be taken up by the Revd. Mr. Stewart and Mr. James Cowan and that the Subject was to be Republic versus Monarchy . . . after which all the Members present took part in the discussion and on the vote being taken Eleven voted for Monarchy and Five for Republic."

Monday the — May 1894. Seems to have been a business meeting when the Treasurer presented his accounts showing a balance of £5;12;6½. The 12/6½ was paid to Mrs. Cameron for cleaning the school after the meetings. Two pounds was to be spent on purchasing books, and Mr. Cameron was appointed Librarian. "Mr. James Christie intimated to the Meeting that he would move at next meeting that the Members get up a Flower and Vegetable Show sometime during this season."

21st. June 1894. "Mr. Osborne stated that he and Mr. Stewart met as requested by the last meeting and made a selection of Thirtysix Books a list of which he had now pleasure of laying before the Meeting for their approval, but the Meeting found that they would need to curtail the list to Twentythree so as not to exceed the ammount of two pounds." Mr. Christie presented several sets of rules for Flower Shows and the meeting appointed a committee of eight members to carry out the necessary arrangements.

The next meeting was not until 29th. October 1894 when members were told that there was a credit balance of £2:17:7. "After some discussion it was arranged to carry on the Winter Meetings fortnightly as last year. The first to be for Members only and to be held on 8th. Nov. and to consist of Songs, Recitations & Readings each member present to take an active part. Rev. P. Stewart was to occupy the Chair. It was further agreed to hold a Public Meeting on the week following. The programme to be sustained by the Members of the Society with the addition of the Magic Lantern." "The Secretary then intimated that he intended to resign and thereby give another Member a chance to act as Secretary. Mr. Gillespie was proposed for the Office. Mr. Gillespie wanted time to consider over it, and promised to let the Secretary know by the end of the week whether he would accept or not." Whether that meeting took place is not recorded and the next minute is not until 21st. January 1895, when it was arranged to have a meeting of members on the Friday following, the 25th. inst. each member to contribute a song, reading or recitation. Two members were appointed to assist the Librarian to catalogue and number the books in the Library and have them ready for distributing at an early date.

25th. January 1895. The meeting took place as arranged; Mr. Christie intimated the books in the Library were now ready for distributing. It was agreed "to give a Magic Lantern entertainment on Friday the 15th. Feb. the committee to meet in Bridgend Hall on Friday the 29th. Jan. to draw out a programme and make arrangements."

There is a note below these minutes which says, "The above entertainment came off on Friday 15th. but owing to the inclemency of the weather the audience was very small." Collection 5/-. After that there is no more and the accounts cease until January 1898 when they were balanced showing a credit of £2:12:7½. We must assume that the Society only operated from 1893 to 1895. The subjects of some of the Magic Lantern entertainments can be ascertained from the account book and include: A thousand miles up the Congo; On Service; How we hunted a mouse; Mary Queen of Scots; and two comics, Nephews and Stolen Sausage; Through the Trossachs; Burns Cottars Saturday Night and How Tammy Tended the Baby; British Empire; Life of General Gordon; and Sermon in Candles.

Twenty-nine volumes, $5\frac{3}{4} \times 3\frac{3}{4}$ ins., whose small print must have been difficult to read by lamp or candle light, have survived and if these are typical of the whole library one might be forgiven, in 1984, for not being surprised by the short life of the Society. They include: A Voyage to Abyssinia by Father Jerome Lobo. Translated by Samuel Johnson; Poems by George Crabbe; Essays by Abraham Cowley; Knickerbocker's History of New York by Washington Irving; Letters on England by Voltaire; Table Talk of Martin Luther; Mankind and Political Arithmetic by Sir William Petty; The Natural History of Selborne by Rev. Gilbert White; The Diary of Samuel Pepys; Seven Discourses on Art by Sir Joshua Reynolds; Sermons on Evil-speaking by Isaac Barrow D.D.; Sermons on the Card and other discourses by Hugh Latimer; The Curse of Kehama by Robert Southey; Trips to the Moon by Lucian. Translated from the Greek by Thos. Franklin; The Black Death and The Dancing Mania by J. F. C. Hecker. Trans. Bebington; The Wisdom of the Ancients and New Atlantis by Francis Bacon, and Four of Shakespeare's plays.

Perhaps the contributor to the "Glasgow Geography" in 1825 writing of the Scottish peasant was correct when he said, "By the time he has reached the age of ten years, he has by heart, as it is called, the whole Catechism, the metrical version of the Psalms, and is pretty well versed in the Bible . . . and by the time he arrives at the years of maturity, to the 'big ha' Bible once his father's pride,' and the Westminister Confession of Faith, he has added Pool, Henry's Commentary, Gillespie's Aaron's Rod Blossoming, the Faithful Contendings of the Church of Scotland, Boston's Fourfold State, and if he can afford them the works of Jonathan Edwards."

COATS LIBRARIES

There may still be a few people in Islay who will remember, no doubt with appreciation, the Coats libraries, a source of firstly recreation and secondly instruction, when books were scarce in the island except in the houses of the proprietors, and to a lesser degree, the doctor, the ministers and the schoolmasters, long before popular newspapers, radio and television were easily available.

When James Coats was touring the Highlands and Islands in his yacht he found that the lighthouse keepers had nothing to read in their off duty periods so he presented a library to every lighthouse round the coast of Scotland. He did the same to the soldiers' barracks and police stations; there may have been time for the policemen to read seventy-five years ago but not today. He found that the country districts of the Highlands were no better off and offered them libraries too.

James Coats, junior (1841-1912), was a member of the Paisley family of industrialists J. & P. Coats, whom most of us know best as the makers of sewing cotton but he appears to have made the presentation of these libraries personally and not through a trust established in connection with the firm. He provided over 300 libraries between 1905 and his death in 1912.

The libraries in the country districts were housed in the schools but a few were in church halls where schools were not available. He chose schools because they were usually the centre of the village activities and he hoped that the schoolmaster as well as taking care of the books would be likely to encourage both his pupils and their parents to read them. The offers were made to the County Council who normally consulted the schoolmaster before accepting and he was a very important factor in their success. Full use of the books was not made in some of the stricter districts of the Highlands where, it is recorded, some teachers refused to read fiction to their pupils because it was "untrue."

The libraries were standardised to some degree. The book cases were made of deal and stained, were six feet high and about five feet six inches wide, in two sections each with glass fronted doors, and had six shelves. The number of books was usually about a hundred but sometimes much larger. Each case carried a small brass plate saying it was presented by James Coats, junior, and each book had a bookplate giving the name of the library, the date of presentation and the book number. They were intended for recreation rather than instruction and supplied by A. Gardner, a bookseller in Paisley, who seems to have had a free hand in their selection, Coats dictating the general policy. They were mainly fiction with many English classics — Dickens, Scott, Thackaray, a set of Encyclopedia, Highland history, biography, and, in the appropriate areas, much Gaelic literature and poetry. There is no evidence that there were ever any lending rules.

There was one major flaw in this inspired scheme, no provision was made for maintenance or replacement. Perhaps it was hoped that being housed in schools the education authority would maintain continuity; none did so.

The books were eagerly borrowed, well used and finally fell to pieces, as was the case with J. F. Campbell's "Popular Tales of the West Highlands" in the Port Ellen library. Stocks became depleted through wear and tear and theft. (I wonder why through the ages so many people steal books? Perhaps we are born with an immense desire for knowledge, which can be obtained from books. When they were hand copied and illuminated they were very rare and valuable, and not much less so in the early days of printing. Has the desire been bred in us or is it that there are so many and so easily available today that they are no longer considered of value?) When all the books had been read the local reader lost interest.

All that remains of the Port Ellen library is the brass plaque and five volumes in the Gaelic which bear the date 1905 and one of them is number 305, so it must have been one of the largest as well as one of the early ones. Of Bruichladdich there are the bookcases which are now in the Islay museum. There are probably a number of books with the Coats bookplate, many in Gaelic, to be found in private collections.

There were libraries in the lighthouses at Portnahaven, Rhuvaal and probably McArthur's Head but I have not been able to find out what happened to them.

A most interesting feature was the employment of Mr D. T. Holmes to visit the Highlands and report on the use made of and the appreciation of the libraries. He did this by undertaking a tour giving literary lectures and talks on elocution and in 1909 he published "A Literary Tour of the Highlands & Islands of Scotland." His account of a visit to Port Charlotte is worth quoting. "It is a weird experience to drive along the shore road from Bridgend on a night of pitiless rain, and see the heavy mists broken every now and then by the far-reaching flash of the Portnahaven lighthouse. Equally weird is it to lecture in a school with no lamps (as happened at Port Charlotte). At eight o'clock I could see the faces of the audience well enough, but by and by the room became quite dark, and I seemed to be addressing an audience of silent and attentive ghosts. After I had finished, a Phantom arose in the far corner of the room and proposed a vote of thanks; and thereafter a Voice somewhere pronounced the benediction. Then there was a movement of feet, and the shadowy spectres trooped out into the night. The foolish virgins had no oil in their lamps; in Port Charlotte, there was neither oil nor lamps."

I am indebted for most of this information to the Librarian of the Renfrew District Library Service in Paisley and the papers of their local history department. Holmes D.T. "Literary Tours of the Highlands and Islands of Scotland" 1909.

Mention should be made of the report of Alfred Barnard when he visited Lagavulin in the 1880s. He writes "Finally we visited the reading room, which Mr Mackie has generously provided for his workpeople and which is well supplied with newspapers and current literature of the day."

There was a small library belonging to the Freemasons' Lodge in Bowmore but this has been disposed of; and possibly other organisations had small collections of specialist books. Another small library of comparatively recent date is the one in the sitting room of the Eventide Homes in Bowmore. When Captain Barclay, of the Scottish Air Ambulance Service, retired, the people of the island made a collection to be presented to him in appreciation of his long service. He asked that out of it books should be provided for the old people. The accompanying plaque reads:—

The David Barclay Library
Presented by
The People of Islay
opened by
Captain David Barclay M.B.E.
of the Scottish Air Ambulance Service
15 December 1965

No provision could be made for the selection of books to be kept up to date and they are not much used now, but there is an excellent service of books from the Argyll and Bute District library for the residents and patients in the hospital.

For some years the local authority sent boxes of books which were changed monthly and which were distributed by volunteers from their homes or village halls on two evenings a week. The annual number of borrowings was about 5,000. In February 1974 a mobile library service was inaugurated and at the end of its first ten years the number of books lent should have grown to nearly twenty times as many. The success of this greatly appreciated service must in a great measure be due to the pleasant and most helpful personality of the librarian.

Industrial Archaeology

IT is, perhaps, expecting too much for every item of industrial archaeology to be mentioned in two volumes which cover the whole of Scotland, and John R. Hume in "The Industrial Archaeology of Scotland," Volume two, The Highlands and Islands, does not explain why only some are selected. This must be considered unsatisfactory.

All the main distilleries are mentioned and, with the exception of Port Charlotte, they are still working. Many of them started as a collection of small bothies at which distilling was taking place. In "The Stent Book" in 1796 and again in 1801 there is a resolution suppressing distilling because the nation is threatened by famine. In 1821 Neill MacEachern & Co. made 6798 gallons of 70 proof at Daill. D. MacEachern Jr. & Co. produced 4480 gallons at Bridgend. Donald McEachern, late merchant & distiller, at Bridgend, died in 1843 and was buried at Kilarrow. This was not the distillery at Newton House which was supplied with water from Loch Skerrols by a lade which ran just inside the wall of the wood below Newton school where J. MacFarlane made 3937 gallons. A. MacDougall made 4183 gallons at Ardbeg and John Johnston 4178 at Lagavullin. Archibald Campbell, also at Lagavullin, made 2193 gallons. D. & J. Johnston produced 1959 at Tallant. On the Rhinns George Montgomery, distiller and tacksman, who died in 1833 aged 44 years and was buried at Bridgend, made 1392 gallons. The smallest was D. MacNicol who produced only 381 gallons, at Ballygrant.

MacNeill Weir in his guide says that about the year 1827 a large distillery was built close to the River Laggan at Mulindry. The remains of a distillery can still be seen in The Kennels at Lossit. McCuaigs made whisky at Upper Cragabus; one at Torrabus used to belong to Coal Ila; and someone distilled at Ardinisle.

The mills at Kilchiaran, Ballygrant, and Eallabus which are mentioned are perhaps the best but there are the remains of many others. A duty payable in meal for having grain ground at the local mill — known as multure — is listed in the earliest known rental of Islay, which is dated 1626.

The "Islay Parliament" agreed in 1755 that the local people should do two days work repairing the road from Kintra to Kenobus Mill.

The mill at Ballygrant is of the nineteenth century but one would expect that there was an older one at Baile Gràna — Grain Township, and one at Cornabus — Corn Farm, comes as no surprise. Mill stones are still at Lagavullin — mill hollow. At Glenegedale there is Driom a mhuillinn — Ridge of the mill and to the north of Port Ellen is Cnoc na Cloiche-muilinn — Millstone Hill — where there are a number of unfinished mill stones cut out of the rocks. An interesting feature of the mill at Lower Glenastle is an earth ramp up to the first floor.

The one at Eallabus is a replacement for one that was burnt down. Is the one at Erlabus where John King, who died in 1854, was miller, the same?

The New Guide to Islay (1911) mentions a mill at Kilarrow; Neil McKay is referred to as of the millhouse, Bowmore. On the Rinns besides the threshing mill mentioned at Kilchiaran, where the wheel and some machinery are still in position, there are the remains of buildings, the goit and broken millstones at Nerabus. At Machrie, Kilchoman, the mill has been made into a house and there was a millstone there which was only about two inches thick; another thin stone was on the south bank of the Saligo river at NR208639, which is not far away. The mill at Kilchoman is of particular interest being constructed from corrugated iron sheets and was erected first at Craigens farm and moved to Kilchoman when the farmer who owned it went there. Tayvullin (Tigh a' Mhuilinn) at Ardnave is a mill house and also, near Gruinart farm, there is Gleann a' Mhuillinn — the Glen of the mill. Octovullin (Ochdamh a' Mhuillinn) is Mill Eighth farm. The meaning of Mulindry is doubtful but would seem to contain an element of "mill." MacAllister, a miller at Ardnish on the Rinns, was named as one of the four men who were taken prisoner on the pirate ship "Bloody Yankee" when she is supposed to have sailed into Lochindaal, in 1813. There are probably still remains of other mills. The only reference to a horizontal mill, or "click mill" would seem to be to one at Balmavicar (Ballyvicar?) and windmills represented only by Loch a' Mhuilinn-Ghaoith — Windmill Loch.

The Reverend John Walker in his "Report on the Hebrides" 1764 and 1771 writes "There is not the smallest appearance of coal in Ila." There is coal in Kintyre and large pieces are sometimes brought up by fishing boats

working locally, so perhaps the old people who say that coal was mined at Daill and used by a local blacksmith in the First World War are correct, although no trace of workings has been found.

There have been smiths for very many years and it seems likely that workings excavated at Killellan by Colin Burgess in 1974 were those of a bronze age smith. In J. F. Campbell's Popular Tales of the West Highlands (XXVIII) there is the story of The Smith and The Fairies which the Rev. Thomas Pattieson told him about a MacEachern at Crosbrig. This traditional story tells of a boy who had been substituted for the smith's own son who had been taken away by fairies. On a night when he had been told that the round green hill where the son was kept would be open he went there protected with a bible, a dirk and a crowing cock and brought him home. For a year and a day the boy did not work and hardly ever spoke but one day when he was watching his father fashion a sword for an important chief he exclaimed "That is not the way to do it" and taking the tools soon made a sword the like of which was never seen before, and so began the famous Islay swords. The walls of this house where the smith lived and made the "Claidheamh Ceann-Ileach" are still to be seen at Caonis gall not far from Kilchoman church.

The smithies mentioned by Hume, Pennycraig — still in use — and Eorrabus are still complete buildings, but so are the ones at Tighnacala, Ballygrant and the one at Port Ellen, which was used up to 1870, and is to be pulled down for road widening. Farms often had their own smithies, as at Kindrochid. One, now a holiday home, is at the entrance to the Kildalton estate.

A stone found in the enclosure round Kintour farmhouse in September 1881 was in the Kildalton Castle collection. It was a rough undressed stone slab 21 ins. × 19 ins., two inches thick, with a hole in the middle about three and a half inches in diameter. Scott and James McCalman said at the time that it was a stone used for making charcoal after the following fashion; a hole was scooped out in the floor of the dwelling, the stone placed over it with the hole being directly above the hollow in the floor. Burning peats were taken from the house fire, put through the hole in the stone into the cavity below, a damp turf was placed on top, and so the charcoal was made. It was the custom for every man, when going to the smithy, to provide his own iron and charcoal.

The present wool mill was built in 1883 from stone quarried from the nearby River Sorn. On the opposite side of the lane, near a bridge over the river, are the remains of a much earlier mill; both were driven by water from the Sorn. Could there have been at sometime a mill in that most attractive valley which runs northeast from the bridge over the burn near Lyrabus? Although there are no visible remains the name persists in Gleann a' chardaidh — Glen of the wool carding.

It was to the old mill that James Christie came from Kintyre, where he worked as a spinner in a lint mill, in 1873 and for ten years carded wool for the local women to spin, did a little weaving and some farming. The ceilings were so low that one wonders how anyone could get at the carding machines to clean them. Just to the east of these mills is the now derelict Waulk Mill cottage. It is said that when Christie moved into the new mill he took the machinery with him and this must have included the scribbler and carder, with the "Devondale" piercing machine, the slubbing Billy and spinning Jennys. There are only two other piecing machines known; one is in store in the Science Museum, London, and the other in Bankfield Museum, Halifax. (See Dr. J. A. Iredale's paper "The last two piecing machines.") The exact date of this one is not known, but they were patented by Robert Archibald in 1858. According to the late Dr. K. R. Gilbert of the Science Museum the slubbing Billy could be unique and he believed that there were only five other Jennys left, all in museums. Mr William B. Christie, the third generation, retired in 1979. The Islay Woollen Mill Co. Ltd. obtained a lease on the mill from Islay Estates and bought the machines from Mr Christie in 1981.

The meal mills and the wool mill found work for a number of millwrights.

The Rinns of Islay Robert Stevenson lighthouse and the Loch Indaal light at Port Charlotte, built in 1869, are recorded but not the others. The one at Rhuvaal at the north of the island was established in 1859. Now they are all automatic. McArthur's Head at the south end of the Sound of Islay was built in 1861 and converted from oil to incandescent in 1907. A much smaller one was established at Carraigh Mhor, south of Port Askaig, in 1928. The one on Chuirn Island at the south east of Islay was established in 1907 and converted from oil to dissolved acetylene in 1911. The memorial harbour light on Carraig Fhada at the entrance to Kilnaughton Bay was built in 1853 and taken over by the Commissioners of Northern Lighthouses in 1924. It was originally an acetylene light but was converted to propane gas operation in 1963.

Valuation of Finlaggan Sheep Stock

				£	s	d	£	s	d
		Proportion of Sheep taken over by Mr. Edward Fletcher Kepposh, on 19th May 1885, as his share for the Farm of Robolls.							
		Ewes & Lambs							
	259⅗	Tops @ £39.10/- each clad score 2 Shotts	£	487	10	10¼ 1/7			
	28⅖	Shotts @ £26.6.8		36	2	3¼ 5/7			
288							523	13	1½ 6/7
		Unlambed Ewes							
	31½	Tops @ £38 „ each clad score 2 shotts		57	„	„			
	3½	Shotts @ £25.6.8		4	4	5¼ 1/3			
35							61	4	5¼ 1/3
		Eild Ewes							
	42	Tops @ £33 „ 10 each clad score no Shotts		67	„	„			
42							67	„	„
		Old Eild Ewes							
	17	Tops @ £12 each clad score no shotts		9	14	3¼ 6/7			
17							9	14	3¼ 5/7
		2 Year old Wedders							
	8	Tops @ £34 each clad score no shotts		12	19	0½ 2/7			
8							12	19	0½ 2/7
		Ewe Hoggs							
	19⅗	Tops @ £36.10/- each clad score 2 Shotts		34	8	3¼ 5/7			
	2⅖	Shotts @ £24.6.8		2	10	11¾ 5/21			
22							36	19	3¾ 20/21
		Wedder Hoggs							
	13	Tops @ £23 „ 10/- each clad score 1 Shott out of lot		14	10	11¼ 5/7			
	1	Shott @ £15 „ 13 „ 4			14	11½ 4/21			
14							15	5	10¼ 19/21
426		Forward	£				726	16	0¾ 1/21

Valuation of Finlaggan sheep stock 1885

IT is not possible to understand this interesting document until it is remembered that it represents a SHARE of sheep taken over and not a public SALE and then fractions of an animal become acceptable.

Tops indicate the top quality and shotts inferior ones; some, for example the two in the first item, are not charged for and were perhaps very poor.

One cannot reconcile the calculation until it is realised that a clad score equals 21, and the treatment of fractions of a penny is individual.

Eild ewes are those which are not in lamb.

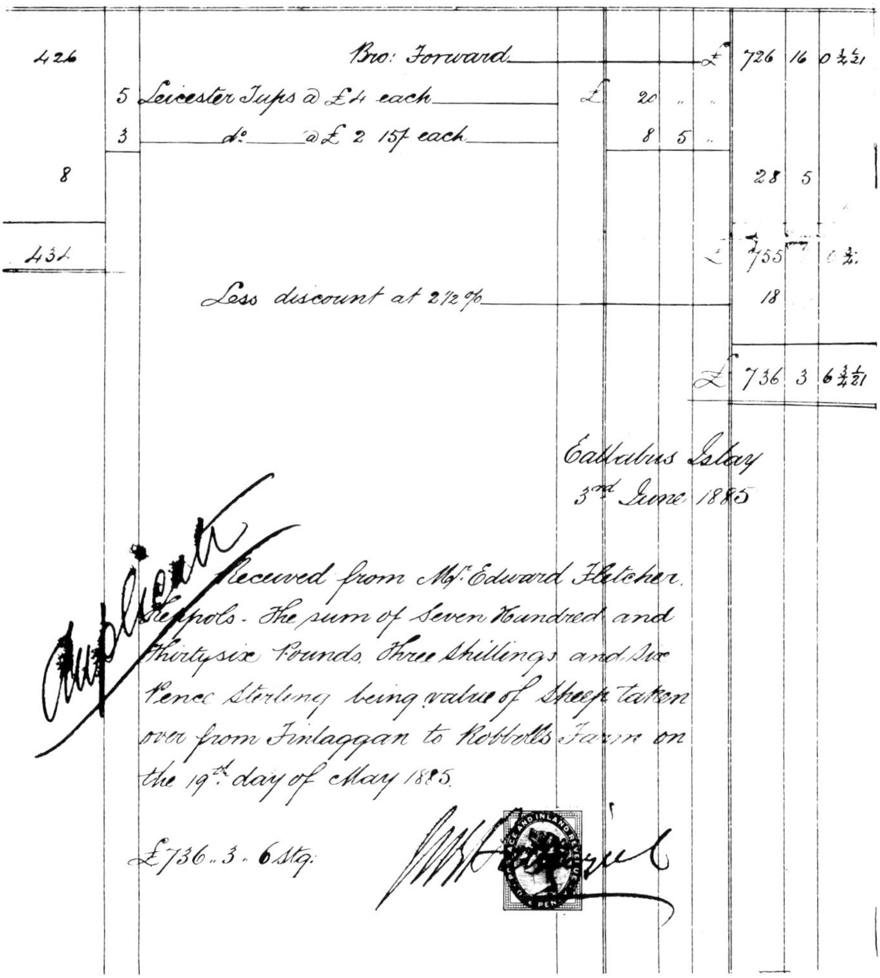

426		Bro: Forward			£	726	16	0 ¾ 1/21
	5	Leicester Tups @ £4 each	£	20	" "			
	3	do @ £ 2 15/- each		8	5 "			
8						28	5	
431					£	755		0 ¾
		Less discount at 2½ %				18		
					£	736	3	6 ¾ 1/21

Eallabus Islay
3rd June 1885

Duplicate

Received from Mr. Edward Fletcher, Keppols. The sum of Seven Hundred and Thirtysix Pounds, Three Shillings and Six Pence Sterling being value of Sheep taken over from Finlaggan to Robolls Farm on the 19th day of May 1885.

£736 .. 3 .. 6 stg.

A letter from the Jura hotel August 1890

IT was written by Mary Edgar to a Mrs Waddell; nothing is known about either of them, but one would like to have known Mary Edgar who could write such a letter. What a contribution they make to our understanding of the past.

"We have just arrived here with everything we have *soaking wet* and so we must just sit still till our clothes are dried and I take the opportunity of the idle time to write to you—

I left home this morning before seven to join the Columba at Greenock. We picked up Miss Rintoul at Kilmalcolm and afterward we had a very pleasant journey till we reached Tarbert Lochfyne. . . . We had been looking forward rather to this little drive between East and West Tarbert, but our greatest pleasure was when we stepped safely down at the pier where the little Islay steamer 'Fingal' was waiting to carry us to this island of Jura.

When we stepped on board we found the boat largely occupied by sheep, always very smelly companions in a steamer. Having secured seats on the saloon deck we went to look about us, and saw another large flock of sheep being driven down the quay towards our steamer. It was interesting to watch the getting of them on board. Two of the drovers took a strip of white cotton about 20 yards long and held it across the top of the quay, and it did for a fence. No sheep offered to pass it. Then of course not one would enter the gangway to go into the steamer, so they caught one and forced it through, then all the rest followed quite eagerly of their own accord. After that lot was safely in, behold another flock drawing near the pier and they all had to be stored in too, one would wonder wherever they packed themselves, imagine our feelings on raising our heads to draw a long breath when the last sheep was in, to find another large flock making its way towards us. It was perfectly absurd. Surely not one more could cram into the sheep quarters, but down they came, and a gangway was placed right on our saloon deck. It was nearly half a minute before we took in the situation, and then it was too ludicrous. Everybody looked at every other body and burst out laughing. One lady, daughter of the proprietor of Jura said to the Captain — 'Captain, do you mean to say you are going to turn us off the only nice place in the steamer and put sheep in it?'

The Captain bowed low and said — 'Even so, madam.'

Then what a scramble there was! Each one seizing his or her bundle of wraps and nearly tumbling over each other on the narrow stair leading down to the cabin deck. The first discovery was that there were very few seats there. A search was made for camp-stools, and about half a dozen were found. I got one, with one of the straps broken. When the luggage was all brought in, we managed to get seated on boxes and bags, etc. It was a relief when we felt ourselves fairly started and we enjoyed the beautiful sail down Loch Tarbert. . . . About an hour before reaching Jura dark clouds began to roll over on us from its lofty peaks, and soon we had a perfect torrent of rain. The sea also began to break over us and wash along the decks. In a short time we were thoroughly drenched and landed in Jura among what felt like 'buckets of water.' We had telegraphed to the Hotel for rooms and there was a fire in the sitting room at which we spent the rest of the evening drying our clothes. The Hotel is a very poor one. We got wretched tea, just like blue water, milk for cream, hard bread and bad butter; we could get nothing but ham and eggs and the ham was so hard we could not eat it. In the course of the evening a note was handed in from Mrs Campbell of Jura House saying she had heard of our arrival and as she was sure there was no comfort in the Hotel she hoped we would come there in the morning and stay with them while we were on the island, assuring us also that she would do all in her power to further the cause for which we had come. This was our first note of encouragement and we were thankful for it, as we had come to the Island on a delicate mission and we needed support."

More detail of the delicate mission would have been enlightening but one can get some idea. Back at the Hotel they "got another horse and gig to take us to Lagg, a distance of nine miles north where our good missionary lives. On our way we called on the established church minister, who had been the means of our coming to the Island, and with whom we had special business, and were immensely tickled to find that he had actually fled! His wife in her innocence told us he had been down at the steamer when we landed and had slipped out of sight, and next morning he had left at six o'clock to go and visit a small island North of Jura where he had never been known to go before."

Then follows a description of their travels on Jura, their meeting with the factor next morning and leaving about noon to cross to Islay.

"We lunched at the Inn at Port Askaig, and being unable to get a hire we secured seats in the post's gig to cross Islay to Bridgend where was a good Hotel in which we intended to pass the night. I had rather a dread of this post's conveyance for it was only a spring cart, and I thought I felt myself being bumped, but as it was I enjoyed this nine miles in the post gig better than all the drives I had had. It was warm sunshine and the seat was easy and the progress slow. Deliciously enjoyable. At Bridgend Hotel everything was first class — grub — rooms — surroundings, but we were knocked up at five o'clock next morning to start by coach at six for Port Ellen in the south of Islay, where we were to join the steamer at half past eight to return home.

We got on the top of the coach. It was cold, but we had plenty of wraps and were so comfortable, and the morning air and sunshine were so refreshing. The distance was eleven miles and we did it in two hours. Then we got on board the little 'Fingal' and soon were joined by a number who had travelled with us when we came and whom we greeted as old friends. Then we got our fears confirmed that there was a heavy sea on; all night long the wind had howled round my room. And I made up my mind — 'Now Mary Edgar you'll be terribly sea-sick,' so I was prepared for the worst. Off we went and the sun shone out and the waves danced and sparkled and our spirits with the sport of the waters. Out we went where the swell of the Atlantic drive was strong and fierce and the little steamer tossed about like a cork. She rose and plunged and rolled and staggered and behaved generally in a most frisky fashion. And what of the poor passengers. O how ill some of them were. Once when we were getting along amazingly, in an instant a huge wave literally stood straight up at our side, then dashed itself on us with vindictive fury. Anything like the commotion that ensued, the hurricane deck and one of the steamer's boats which was hung aloft broke its range so far, but some ladies who had got settled on that side had to be led down stairs dripping wet. We got wetted, everyone got wetted, but that was nothing. The worst bit was to come, when the steamer rolled over and took in water over her bulwarks at one side, then rolled straight over and took in water over her bulwarks at the other side. We found it safer to hold on with two hands then. Well, we got through it all, I can scarcely believe that I came through all that and thoroughly enjoyed the excitement of it, and was not in the least bit sea-sick. The remainder is not worth telling. The usual sail up in the 'Columba,' the story is absurdly long already."

Island of Islay in 1825

as described in "The Scotsman's Library" by James Mitchell, LL.D. 1825.

ABOUT forty-five years ago there was no carriage road, and not above two or three carts in the whole island of Islay. There are now ninety miles of carriage road in different directions, and above 500 carts. At that time, green crops and sown grasses were almost absolutely unknown, and very little natural hay secured for winter use. At present every tenant makes as much hay as supports his stock in winter; and has not only potatoes, cabbages, and meal in abundance for his family, but also frequently sells corn and potatoes, and feeds his cattle up to a third more weight than his predecessors were wont to do. Most of the gentlemen farmers have turnips, rye-grass, and clovers in great perfection, and the smaller tenants are anxious to follow their example. The cultivation of wheat was, until very lately, never thought of in Islay; but Mr. Campbell of Shawfield, and several of his more opulent and adventurous tenants, now raise considerable quantities annually, and find it to answer astonishingly well. It is probable that the species commonly called summer or spring wheat will continue to be the favourite sort of this grain; and although the cultivation of it may not perhaps be advisable in general over the Hebrides, yet, in consequence of various circumstances favourable to it in Islay, and especially the building of a flour mill by the enlightened and patriotic proprietor, (which cost him £1200), this valuable crop may be extended over a large portion of the best farms in the island. Several thousand bolls of potatoes, and considerable quantities of barley, are exported yearly; perhaps, indeed, too much of the last-mentioned crop, in consequence of the great demand from the opposite coast of Argyle and Kintyre for the purpose of distillation. The proprietor, however, does all in his power to prevent smuggling and every species of clandestine and illegal operations in grain, and in every other commodity, fully aware of the bad consequences resulting from these to many of the most fertile Hebrides. He has accordingly built, in the heart of Islay, the only brewery in the Western Isles, for preventing the evils alluded to, and for gradually weaning off his tenants from a taste for ardent spirits, and accustoming them to the more nourishing and wholesome beverage of ales; and has, by these means, not only improved the agriculture, but also the morals of the island.

Free Church of Scotland, Presbytery of Islay 1843 to 1900

Extract From
ANNALS OF THE FREE CHURCH OF SCOTLAND
1843 - 1900
Edited by W. Ewing, D.D.

XXVIII
PRESBYTERY OF ISLAY

BOWMORE After the Disruption in 1843, occasional services were arranged for Bowmore in connection with Killarrow. In 1856 it was recognised as a preaching station. It was sanctioned as a Church Extension charge in 1859. Church and manse were erected in 1860, and a school soon afterwards. The congregation were greatly indebted to Claud Macfie of Gogarburn, and Charles McNeil, one of the elders, for counsel and help. In 1874 the widow of the latter, carrying out her husband's wishes, left £1650, the annual interest of which to be applied to augment the minister's stipend. Mr. Macfie also gave £400, the annual interest to be credited to the Sustentation Fund of the congregation.

Membership: 1861, 25; 1900, 51.

Ministers: 1. Hugh Munro, 1860-1869. 2. Alexander Mackintosh, 1874-1879. 3. P. McIver, 1882-1900.

KILCHOMAN (PORT CHARLOTTE) Alexander Cameron, minister of the parish, "came out" in 1843. A new church was erected forthwith. The manse was built in 1847. The parish is large and the population sparse. The gradual decline of the latter adversely affected the congregation.

Membership: 1848, 52; 1900, 71.

Ministers: 1. Alexander Cameron, 1843-1872. 2. James MacMillan, 1873-1900.

KILDALTON AND OA Many people in Port Ellen adhered to the Free Church in 1843, and a congregation was immediately formed, although some years elapsed before a minister was settled. The Church was built in 1845, outside Port Ellen, on a hill overlooking the village. The manse was erected in 1848.

Membership: 1848, 65; 1900, 86.

Ministers: 1. Alexander Mackenzie, 1847-1871. 2. Alexander Lee, M.A., 1872-1875. 3. Donald McMaster, 1876-1896. 4. Daniel Munro, 1896-1900.

KILLARROW AND KILMENY The minister and many of the congregation of the quod sacra church of Kilmeny "came out" in 1843; and were joined by those who left the parish church of Killarrow. The new church was built at Skerrols, and opened in February, 1844. The manse was erected in 1846. The rural population considerably declined. The members and adherents from Bowmore and its vicinity were disjoined in 1859, and made a separate charge.

Membership: 1855, 215*; 1900, 32.

Ministers: 1. James Pearson, 1843-1883. 2. Peter Stewart, 1881-1900.

PORTNAHAVEN After some hesitation the minister of the parish remained in the Establishment in 1843. All the elders and a large proportion of the people "came out" in July, and a congregation was formed. School and teacher's house were erected in 1849. The congregation had the status of a station under Kilchoman. Under Dr. McLachlan's scheme an endowment of £1,000 was gathered before 1875, in which year the charge was sanctioned. School and teacher's house were then renovated and enlarged and became church and manse. A new manse was erected in 1892, and the church was repaired in 1893.

Membership: 1876, 123*; 1900, 69.

Ministers: 1. John G. McNeil, 1875-1885. 2. Angus McDonald, 1886-1890. 3. A. S. McIntyre, B.D., 1891-1900.

* Approximate figures.

Free Church, Port Charlotte.

Free Presbyterian Church of Killarrow and Kilmeny 1843 to 1916

FROM THE SESSION BOOK OF
THE FREE PRESBYTERIAN CHURCH
OF KILLARROW AND KILMENY
1843 - 1916

THE book opens with a declaration signed by each Elder and Deacon as elected, followed by the 23 chapters of the Confession of Faith. At the first meeting there is set out in full the Protest by Ministers and Elders of 18th May 1843, and the Act of Separation and Deed of Demission by Ministers.

Most of the meetings are for the purposes of electing Elders and Deacons; selecting dates for Communion and purging and adding to the roll in preparation; electing a representative in the Presbytery and Synod; and acting as a court of discipline. The number of cases for discipline decrease but there is still the occasional case of antenuptial fornication up to the closure of the book in 1916.

The following abstracts from the Session minutes are taken to illustrate their work.

16-6-1843 "Considering that within the bounds of this parish there is not such a number of adherants, as would of themselves form a Congregation, but that it is necessary that the parish of Bowmore, or part of it at least, should be united with this parish under one Kirk session, they associate with them as a member of Session."

14-5-1844 "The Session considering that James Gibson, under process for the crime of fornication, (with Ann Darroch), has submitted to the discipline of the Church, appeared publically and been rebuked before the congregation, and hoping from the professions he now makes, as well as the readiness with which he submitted to discipline, that he is penitent, do now absolve him from censure and admit him to the enjoyment of privileges."

12-7- They dealt with "Mary Trotter who before joining the Free Church has been guilty of antenuptial fornication and that while a communicant."

They also "took up the case of Archibald McGreggor, Beadle, of whom an account of a fall from a horse while attending a funeral, a surmise had gone abroad that he was in a state of intoxication" but they found that "nothing could be made a ground of process against him." Lauchlan Galbraith was found "guilty of a relapse in fornication."

16-7- Duncan McGilvray, a Deacon, who had been seen publicly in a state of intoxication was ordered to be publicly rebuked.

3-8- The Session distributed tokens to fourteen communicants. They refused tokens to Donald McCorquodale for being intoxicated in Bowmore,

Mary McNiven of Barr for "selling whisky without licence to companies holding merry meetings and balls in the place," and Williume Johnson for "being negligent in attending public worship."

28-7-1845 John McVorran and Elizabeth Ross were purged from the communion roll for "anticipated fornication."

2-5-1846 "considering the great evils from tippling houses, and also the number of these licensed, judged it proper to bring the matter before the Justices of the Peace by Petition that they might use their power in surpressing as many as possible and refuse to increase the number."

30-7- Hugh Fletcher was "suspended from priviliges at this time being found in a quarrelsome company at an unreasonable hour."

12-1-1847 The Session approved "the faithful stand which the Directors of the Edinburgh and Glasgow Railway Company have made for preserving the sanctity of the Sabbath, by their resolution to discontinue running their carriages on that Holy day.

17-6-1848 They forwarded "a memorial to Lord John Russell praying that the Post Office should be caused to be shut throughout the Kingdom on the Lord's day; and on 19th February 1849 they petitioned the shareholders at Perth against running trains on the Sabbath.

27-10-1851 The Session were having difficulty in clearing the manse debt and decided to take a monthly collection at the church door until it was cleared.

18-12- Donald Sutherland, congregational school teacher, was appointed Session clerk, unpaid.

30-8-1856 John Campbell, publichouse keeper, was struck off the Communion Roll the authorities having fined him for "keeping his house open at unreasonable hours."

18-10- Recognition of Mulindry school which for "a short time and special purpose" had been considered the Congregational School, was withdrawn.

18-4-1865 The Session learned that a new attempt was being made to have the Royal Botanic Gardens open on the Sabbath and petitioned Parliament to refuse the grant.

26-12- James McDermid, shepherd at Lossit, applied for baptism of his child. The Session had been told that "he had gone in company with some others and killed a deer in Jura" and that he "unnessarily frequented a public house" and decided that he should be admonished before the Session. It is not recorded whether they agreed to baptise the child.

28-8-1866 Norman McLeod, an Elder, had ceased to attend public worship for the last year and two other Elders were sent to find out why, "when he assigned as reasons several charges against the Minister, that his preaching was neither law nor Gospel; that he considered him aiming at himself personally in his preaching." He resigned the office of Elder.

23-7-1867 Duncan Fletcher was suspended because "he had in public manner brought reproach on the profession of the Gospel by an unbridled tongue."

23-7-1870 Catherine Williams, a member of the Welsh Calvinist Church in Manchester, was given a communion token.

7-10-1874 The trustees of the late James Bannatyne had made a grant of £100 to assist in employing a Catechist and the money "was lodged with the Greenock Board of Police at 4% interest, to be drawn as required. (The grant was repeated in 1876 and lodged in the National Bank, Bridgend).

12-10- There was a proposal that it was desirable to have "an assistant to labour in the district by preaching and visiting" and it was thought that Mr Findlay of Dunlossit would give assistance towards this object. It was reported on

16-11- that he would contribute £50 and proposed that services should be held at Keills and Ballygrant alternately at the usual hours of public worship on the Sabbath. The Session would not agree to the time; and that seems to have been thc end of it.

23-3-1875 The attention of the Session was drawn to "the desirability of having the children brought together on the Sabbath in a central place" and they agreed to give the subject further consideration.

On 10-5- they found "that for the present at least no arrangement preferable to the present appeared practicable."

20-3-1877 Duncan McLugash, Elder, confessed "that having been led to use a little whisky for relieving asthmatic tightening of the chest, he regrets that he incautiously allowed himself to go to excess, whereby he was overcome by it."

He was suspended from office and appeared before the congregation for public rebuke.

13-10-1879 John McLeod, a policeman residing at Ballygrant, was added to the communion roll.

23-12- The Rev. James Pearson wrote that "finding that my age and growing infirmities render me unable to continue to discharge the duties" he was asking the General Assembly to appoint a successor. He had been unable to preach since July last. He died 19 January 1883 aged 82 and in the 54th year of his ministry.

3-11-1881 The Rev. Peter Stewart was inducted.

15-7-1882 The communion roll contained 59 names.

4-1-1883 It was resolved to form a Total Abstinence Society within the congregation.

6-2- "That whilst under the Old Testament Instrumental Music was prescribed as part of the Temple service it was removed along with the other peculiarities of that service, under the new and more spiritual dispensation from which ritualistic and sensuous forms of worship were excluded; that no Instrumental Music was prescribed or practised by Christ and his Apostles. . . . May it therefore please the General Assembly to withold all sanction to the introduction of Instrumental Music into our worship."

30-3-1884 Alex McLeod, Lightkeeper, Rhuvaal Lighthouse stated that he had fallen into the sin of fornication but he desired the privilege of baptism of his child.

30-3-1885 "Four minutes in reference to the case of Dugald Campbell and Mr Alex McConnely and relative papers are ordered to be kept in a separate record."

5-4-1887 "The Session resolved to petition the Government in favour of the entire abolition of the Acts for the State Regulation of Vice in the Crown Colonies" and in 1894, in India.

August 1891 The communion roll was 38 and in 1894. 33 in 1897, 1899 and 1902. 29 in 1904.

4-4-1900 The minister had to go to Rhuvaal to baptise Donald McDonald's child.

2-10-1905 They discussed the report of the Synod Committee and were dissatisfied, the report being "a misrepresentation of the state of the congregation" and expressed their sympathy with Rev. Peter Stewart and assured him of their full confidence. But on.

17-11- In the Public Hall at Bridgend, the Moderator expressed his sympathy with the congregation "on account of their Pastor, Mr Stewart, having resigned and joined the legal Free Church." Then they agreed that Mr Stewart should have the use of the church from twelve to two pm and the United Free Church service to begin at two o'clock.

20-4-1906 For the Communion on 6th May it was arranged that the Rev. D. Munro would preach on the Fast Day (the Thursday before), the Rev. D. J. McInnes would take the Gaelic service on the Sabbath and the Rev. A. McLaren Young of Southend, Campbeltown the English services. The communion roll was 21; 31 in 1909 and 27 in 1911.

30-8-1907 "the Sustentation Fund Committee intimated that the Vacancy Shedule was passed at the minimum of £60.

12-11- "It is hereby certified that Mr James Fraser M.A. preacher of the Gospel was ordained and inducted to the pastoral charge of the Killarrow and Kilmeny congregation by the United Free Church Presbytery of Islay on the 24th October 1907."

13-1-1908 A Feu Charter of the Church, Manse and Glebe at Skerrols had been granted by Charles Morrison Esq. of Islay to the United Free Church congregation for an annual payment of £2.

7-10- "The Session had under consideration the more frequent celebration of the Lord's Supper in the congregation than at present, which is once a year in May and resolved the ordinance be observed on the first Sabbath of November next. . . ." They discussed the desirability of the congregation standing during praise at the English service and recommended that this attitude be adopted. The Moderator intimated his intention of conducting during the winter a singing class in connection with the congregation for the practice of the Psalter and Hymnary.

2-11-1911 As "it was impossible for the congregation to meet on the Sabbath the 5th day of November owing to the stormy weather prevailing that day" they resolved to dispense the Lord's Supper on the next Sabbath.

19-1-1914 The Church Hymnary was introduced in addition to the Psalms and Paraphrases at present in use.

18-1-1915 "The Session had under consideration the question of the running of the public motor bus for pleasure on the Sabbath Day on certain occasions last summer, and the probability that such facilities may be increased this year, and instructed the Moderator to bring the matter to the notice of the Presbytery, with a View to the Presbytery taking such action as they may deem advisable to prevent such encroachment of the Lord's Day.

2-11-1916 The book closes.

Free Church of Scotland, Bowmore; minute book 1858 to 1910

12-1-1858 Opens with a petition to the Committee for the Highlands. "That the population of the parish and village of Bowmore amounts to about three thousand souls; and that of all the population not more than three hundred regularly attend church.

That there is no resident minister at present officiating in the Established Church, and only occasional services held there by the various members of the Presbytery, and that there is no other regular ministry held there by any other denomination of Christians whereby any adequate surveillance might be held over the moral and religious state of the community, and that consequently the sins of intemperance, Sabbath desecration, and the other vices that follow in their train have become sadly prevalent and daily increasing.

That the Free Church congregation are burdened with the expense of maintaining a place of Worship, while they have no minister to occupy it, — Sermon being held there only during two Sabbaths for upwards of three months.

That the congregation progressed favourably during the time they had ministers and probationers to preach there, but their progress has been suddenly arrested by having no minister to officiate among them. And from the same cause Collections for some of the schemes of the Church have not been made.

That the community in general are favourable to the ministrations of the Free Church in preference to any other if they could only obtain them regularly.

That the petitioners beg earnestly to press the consideration of these circumstances upon the Presbytery in the hope that they shall use every effort to obtain services of some servant of Christ who may promote his cause among so neglected and spiritually destitute a community, to which perhaps a parallel will not be found in the Highlands of Scotland."

3-8- The Free Presbytery of Islay met and resolved to constitute themselves a Kirk Session, and on 30-10 did so again, considered nominations and elected Neil McNeill of Laggan and Charles McNeill of Lossit elders. "From this resolution of the Presbytery Mr Pearson asked to leave the chair, which was granted, to enter his dissent so far as regards Mr Charles McNeill."

1-11- A Kirk Session was constituted in Bowmore and "thereafter they proceeded to the usual place of worship of the Free Church, when Mr Cameron preached in the Gaelic and English languages."

1-3-1859 The Convener read the following letter "from Claud McFie Esquire with reference to a donation of £400 which he had given to the

Aged and Infirm Ministers' Fund and a like sum to the Supplementary Sustentation Fund and in reference to which he reserved power to demand the interest during his life; that he was anxious to promote the prosperity of the new Church of Bowmore in Islay, and now desired to appropriate the interest of the latter sum for five years, for that charge, and on this being complied with he gave up for that period his claim for the interest of the former sum, viz £400, to the Aged and Infirm Ministers' Fund."

28-1 At a congregation meeting they "resolved that, as under present circumstances the Spiritual and moral interests of the congregation and the large outlying population cannot be adequately attended to while Bowmore remains a mere station of the church, seeing that when probationers and Deputies of the Church come their stay is but temporary and quite insufficient for the necessities of the place, that an effort be made to raise the contributions of the congregation to an amount which might warrant the Presbytery to recommend to the Assembly that Bowmore be made a regularly sanctioned charge.

That the Presbytery be requested to take this matter into their favourable consideration, pass their judgement thereon, transmit it to the proper quarter and in every way in their power forward the interests and wishes of the congregation towards obtaining the sanction of the General Assembly.

The regular adherents of the congregation are about 100; the average attendance from 150 to 200, and the number of members as far as can be ascertained about 25, but this can form no criterion of what the congregation may become under a regular and thorough ministry." A list of contributions totalling £106 a year is then shown.

4-4 They were unaware that they should have filled in a Schedule for Erection of New Charges but now did so. It appears that "the Free Church in the year 1855 and since that time have worshipped in a loft over a stable — the supply of ordinances has been irregular but the attachment of the adherents of the Free Church has been steadfast." There was no school in connection but one was proposed and a salary provided for the schoolmaster. There was a school about three miles away, at Mulindry.

6-4 The Presbytery met and approved heartily of the application. The General Assembly meeting on 31st May sanctioned Bowmore as a Ministerial Charge.

There is a copy of the Church of Scotland Building Committee schedule which shows that the ground for the church was given free by Charles Morrison with a nominal feu duty.

It shows that the total cost was to be £650 and that a Grant of £300 had been received from a private Debt Extinction Fund subscribed by a few individuals to assist poor congregations.

17-7- Donald Sutherland, Mulindry and Lauchlan Currie, Lossit, were elected Deacons.

20-6-1860 It was understood that Mr Sutherland intended to resign from the school at Mulindry and the Moderator was instructed to look out for a successor.

18-7 James McDonald, a servant at Islay House, asked for baptism for his child and this brought the first case of antenuptial fornication. They determined that the Lord's Supper should be celebrated on the first Sabbath in August.

12-5-1861 Six Deacons were elected. The celebration of the Lord's Supper was to be on 28th July.

27-7 They purged the communion roll leaving 43 members. Mr Sutherland was removed. He protested and his protest was considered on 2-8-1862 when the minute of removal was cancelled. "The Moderator laid on the table a letter dated 4th July which he had received from Mr Sutherland and which having been read was by unanimous order of the Session thrown over the table."

14-5-1863 "The court took into consideration the expediency of proceeding with the erection of a manse and unanimously resolved to request Claud McFie Esq. to let them draw the funds lodged by him."

4-8-1864 Miss Stewart, a governess at Springbank, was added to the roll.

6-9 Mrs Holliday, Bowmore, applied for the baptism of her daughter in the absence of her husband who was on a voyage to Africa and not expected to return for a year, and as they were "satisfied with Mrs Holliday's knowledge as to the ordinance and the obligation" they agreed.

13-6-1865 They appointed the first Sabbath in August for the dispensation of the Lord's Supper and remonstrated with the Kirk Session in Kilmeny who had chosen the same day for their celebration. This correspondence continued for some years until 1878 when they moved to late in June.

22-2-1866 The Session wished to appoint Mr McPhail of H.M. Customs and Mr McIntyre, sergeant of police, Deacons, but Mr McPhail declined and the sergeant had to consult his superiors. In the end neither was appointed.

23-8-1871 The Session suspended Mrs McLugash on this occasion from church privileges for very irregular attendance at public worship during the past year.

5-12-1877 "It was considered whether it would not be for the advantage of the congregation to hold the services on the Sabbath in the school house during the winter months where they could have the comfort of a fire. After some consideration it was unaminously agreed to remain in the church and to take means of getting the church heated and made otherwise comfortable."

16-4-1879 "The Moderator asked Mr Archibald Currie, Elder, to make a statement as to the reports about a disagreement between himself and his son and his son's wife. He made a statement and the Session without passing any opinion in the meantime agree to summon all the parties concerned to a meeting of the Session.

30-4- "The court met to take up consideration of Archibald Currie's case. It was unanimously resolved to delay the case for some time."

15-9- "The meeting proceeded to take into consideration what steps should be taken with the view to electing a minister."

2-12 A sub committee met and put forward four names.

On 10 March 1880 the committee reported to the congregation.

6-8-1880 Archibald Currie etc appeared and "mutually acknowledged that they had been guilty of quarrelling some time ago in a way scandalous to religion in the community where they reside. They expressed deep regret and promised henceforth to keep the peace." Which satisfied the Session.

20-4-1881 The presbytery had appointed two Assessors with the Kirk Session, on account of its present weak state.

5-9- "There was laid on the table a minute of the Deacons' Court of date from which it appeared that the subject of the conversion of the Schoolhouse into dwelling houses had been under consideration, and that the Court had agreed to submit the proposal to the congregation for its opinion."

20-4-1882 Mr Peter McIvor took his seat as Moderator, this being the first meeting of Session after his ordination.

29-3-1883 "The Session resolved to petition the General Assembly against the use of instrumental music in public worship. A petition was read and signed on the spot for that purpose."

7-11-1885 They appointed a day (Thursday) of thanksgiving for the harvest.

13-10-1888 An Assembly Deputation from the Committee on Religion and Morals was to spend a week in Bowmore.

5-12-1891 The Moderator intimated that he intended for the winter months, instead of the ordinary Sabbath evening services, to devote that time as usual to the teaching of a Bible class."

12-3-1892 The classes were not held "owing to the amount of sickness in the district."

7-1-1893 The Session took into consideration the office of Precentor Gaelic and English 23-9- Mr Brodie, tailor, was invited to take the office of English Precentor at a fixed salary. 5-5-1895 they appointed a Precentor for the Gaelic services at the old salary of £2-10-0 per annum.

25-9-1897 The Session had under consideration the subject of having a half yearly Communion and arranged for a service on 7th November.

3-11-1898 "The Moderator read the following extract minute of Presbytery; 'The presbytery took up the report of the committee on union with the United Presbyterian Church as sent down by last General Assembly, and as instructed by the Assembly, agreed to transmit the said report to the Kirk Session within their bounds for their information'."

10-12 "After consideration it was unanimously agreed that the Session see no cause to come to any findings upon the report meantime."

5-5-1900 "The Session, along with Messrs Taylor and Mitchell, Deacons, had the subject of the approaching Union with the United Presbyterian Church under consideration. As this matter has been before the Church for Years, and the various steps necessary for the completion of the Union have already been taken, according to the laws of this Church, and the 31st day of October fixed for the Consummation of the Union, all present cordially approved of the Union taking place on that day."

11-2-1903 The Moderator intimated that owing to the state of his health he was no longer able to perform all his duties and resolved to ask the General Assembly for a grant from the Aged and Infirm Ministers' Fund to aid in securing the services of an unordained assistant.

6-6 The Session agreed that the choir should sit in front of the pulpit along with the Precentor instead of in one of the church pews as formerly.

9-8-1904 "The Session had a conference regarding the situation created by the decision of the House of Lords in the Church Case. The Session regretted their decision and its consequences to the Church, but expressed the hope that both parties may come to some arrangement that the work of the Church shall be carried on without hindrances."

24-9- "The Session desires to record in their minutes the following resolution annent the Church question, viz. that they resolve unanimously to adhere to the union of 1900. And they declare anew their continuous loyalty to the United Free Church in the present crisis." A copy of this resolution was sent to the Advisory Committee.

19-10- There was a further declaration in similar terms.

13-1-1906 They had under consideration the question of using the Hymnary in the public worship and agreed to use it in the summer if there was no serious objection among the people.

11-4-1908 The Session resolved to petition Parliament in favour of the Licensing Bill at present before the House.

10-10 The Session approved of the formation of a Young People's Guild in the congregation.

16-2-1910 The Moderator again asked that application should be made for leave to call a colleague and successor.

20-6 Mrs McIver, wife of the Moderator, asked to be relieved of the duty of leader of praise which she had undertaken for the past two years. "The Session find that there is no suitable person to undertake the duties of precentor, and that they are now in the same position as they were two years ago, when Mrs McIver took up the work. After careful deliberations on the whole situation the Session are unanimously of the opinion that the only satisfactory solution is to be found in the introduction of instrumental music."

21-7- "Letters were read from the secretary and convener of the Praise Committee of the Church with regard to a grant for assisting the congregation to secure an instrument to be used in congregational praise, from which it appears that the Committee were prepared to give £10 on condition that the instrument would be introduced in connection with public worship, and that the congregation contributed a suitable proportion of the cost." The congregation would contribute £8.

16-8- It was agreed to purchase from Paterson & Sons a second hand Harmonium at £20.

The Rev. Roderick Mackenzie was inducted on 9th March 1911.

Islay notes from the Coleraine Chronicle 1876 & 1877

IT is not known who the Islay Correspondent was but the date line was always at Port Ellen. After studying the contributions it would not be unreasonable to conclude that he was Captain Ramsay's factor.

The state of the weather has always been of great interest and almost every column has a full account. Other items appearing regularly include an account of the shipping calling, reports of the meetings of the School Boards, the activities of the 7th Argyll and Bute Volunteers, reports of accidents, and meetings of natives in Glasgow. One might be surprised to find a series of long letters extending over many weeks on Ossian and the Clyde. Information about day to day life in Islay at that time is scarce so I have selected from those columns a variety of interesting occurrences.

1-1-1876 He reports that the harvest had been very abundant but mentions nothing but potatoes, the surplus of which was being sent to the south, the earlies at £5 per ton which after deducting freight etc. leaves the farmer about £4-5-0; rocks were £4 per ton.

The death is reported of A. Shanks at Port Askaig where he had been agent for the steamer "Islay" for over 20 years. His remains were taken by the "Islay" to Port Ellen for burial at Kilnaughton. He had just resigned in order to take charge of his mother's farm at Port Ellen when he died.

The Kildalton Masonic Lodge No. 552 held their annual election, then the Lodge was closed and the brethren marched in procession by torch light through the village. At 7 o'clock the office bearers, a number of the brethren and their lady friends sat down to a sumptuous repast in a granary tastefully decorated with evergreen and flags and after a long toast list the tables were removed for dancing.

The esteemed landlord, John Ramsay Esq., M.P. for the Falkirk Boroughs is reported as "just now receiving a very fair share of abuse from a number of Scottish newspapers, some on personal grounds, others political." The trouble seems to have been based on a report by an Inspector of Schools. Mr Ramsay said they "take advantage of their official position and avail themselves of a report on a school in order to publish their views of the sanitary state of the village in which the school is established, and to offer an opinion regarding the management of an estate of which that village forms a part." His answer was that the village was in no worse state than when he bought the estate and that he had spent over £3000 on improvements though the villagers were legally liable to the cost. As for his neglect of education in Islay, he maintained four schools at his own cost before he owned an acre of land in Islay and that in Port Ellen where the most important of these was he had paid the salary of the teacher for 22 years. He described the charges as "an ebullition of political animosity or personal spite appearing in the Glasgow News."

22-1 The children of the Port Ellen day schools — male and female — with the Sabbath scholars, marched in procession with flags flying to the parish schoolhouse where Mr and Mrs Ramsay had prepared a treat for them. There was a Christmas tree and presents of books or toys and, as they left, each was presented with a bag which contained an orange, sweeties and raisins. On New Year's Day Mr and Mrs Ramsay entertained about 130 old people to a dinner of mutton, venison pies and dessert. Each was given ¼ lb of tea, 2 lbs sugar, a loaf of bread and an article of warm clothing to take home.

The 7th A.A. Volunteers held a dinner and ball at the White Hart. The piper was Alex McKay.

5-2 Another gift was recorded; that of Mrs and Miss McTavish, widow and daughter, now residing in Mull, of the late Rev. Mr McTavish for many years minister at Kildalton. Tea, sugar, soup and bread were given to 54 people.

Although a number of influential parties had been trying to have New Year's Day changed from the old style 13th of the month to 1st, the majority of the natives were loath to change and both days were partially observed.

There was a fire at the home of Dugald Morrison at Leoribus where his daughter and a child lived with him. Nobody was hurt but the thatched roof, and a quantity of hay and peat were destroyed.

The new proprietors of the "Islay," D. Hutcheson & Co. had erected a large new sectional waiting room on the quay. Willie McFarlane "one of the most obliging stewards that ever sailed the seas" retired.

19-2 A meeting of the Water Committee was held at which the principal business was the handing over of money collected. Mr Ramsay promised to give a pound for every one raised by subscription.

A horse and cart belonging to Peter Carmichael, employed discharging coal, went over the breast and into the water between the "Eclipse" and the quay. Both were recovered little worse.

4-3 The new tenant at the farms of Brahunisary and Tyndrum, Roderick Brown, was the recipient of a complimentary day's ploughing by 18 teams.

The Water Committee accepted the tender from D. M. Nelson of Glasgow.

18-2 The death is reported of Robert Ballingall, the Islay Estates factor at the age of 49.

1-4 Malcolm MacKinnon, an old man, was lost in a storm between Bridgend and Mulindry where he lived and a week later had not been found.

Most of the cases at the Sheriff Court were for assault, breach of the peace, trespassing in pursuit of game and one of shebeening (unlicensed selling of liquor).

15-4 The body of Malcolm MacKinnon was found near Schouler on

Daill farm and it was remarkable that it had not been found sooner as it was lying in the vicinity of a well from which water was being drawn daily.

The Oa farmers gave James Hudson, Glenastle, their annual day's ploughing.

22-4 The first meeting of the Killarrow and Kilmeny School Board was held at the Bridgend Hotel.

13-5 A long letter from Hector McLean, Ballygrant, re "Ossian and the Clyde" appears. The first meeting of the Kilchoman School Board took place in Port Charlotte when there was disagreement about opening the meeting with a prayer. The three Established Church representatives set themselves against; the other four who were Free Churchmen were for it. Robert Wilson had "an irresistible tendency to reclaim land" at Laoirinn and reclaimed some 600 acres on this farm. He had nine boilers of 200 gallons each for cooking food for cattle and horses.

27-5 A reply to Hector McLean from P. Hately Waddell started a long correspondence. A fine lot of 46 four-year-old prime Highland bullocks were shipped from Port Ellen by Peter Carmichael from Ballymonie and caused a lot of trouble. When loading them Neil McCuaig fell into the sea and John Fraser was severely struck on the leg and disabled from duty.

1-7 A powerful crane was building a new quay at Ardbeg distillery and a diver was laying the outer walls. It was expected that there would be 13 feet of water during the lowest tides.

12-7 There was another letter from Hector McLean, and by 5 August several other correspondents had joined this controversy.

A party from the Ordnance Survey left after having been stationed here for the last six months.

5-8 Field grown new potatoes were selling at one shilling per stone of 14 lbs, but owing to the abundance of grass there were few cattle at the Bridgend July market.

2-9 William Allan of Sunderland, a poet of no mean rank, had written a drama "Ian Vor" the chief incidents of which are made to occur at Dunyveg in Islay in 1807.

16-9 The steamer "Maggie" brought a quantity of dynamite for use at the Ballygrant lead mines, where a rich and thick lode had been found on the farm of Finlaggan.

A Welsh miner and his wife were on passage on the "Islay" to Port Askaig to join the workers at Ballygrant when his wife was taken ill. Other passengers helped to erect a tent of tarpaulins on the deck and in it she gave birth to a daughter.

W. Dunlop, farmer of Knockdon for the past twelve years, left Bridgend after a market and took a short cut across the sands of Lochindaal and was drowned.

21-10 The "Islay" landed a very fine lot of two-year-old Galloway cattle which he had bought at Falkirk for D. Johnston at Laphroaig.

During this month there was still more correspondence on the Ossianic controversy.

4-11 The "Islay" with a load of barley ran alongside the new quay at Ardbeg for the first time. The screw steamer "Valentia" shipped a cargo of hay for Ballachulish.

11-11 The new schoolhouse at Kintour was progressing rapidly. The contractor for the joinery work was John Kirk of Bowmore.

18-11 Mrs McFarlane resumed her winter evening sewing and knitting classes for grown up girls and young women, in the female schoolroom.

25-11 Dr St. Clair, who used to practice in Islay before he went to Blackpool, was the guest of J. C. Graham at Lagavulin.

At the November market at Bowmore the wages for both male and female servants were reported high.

9-12 Rev; Donald McMaster from Back, Stornoway was inducted to the Free Church at Port Ellen.

16-12 Rev. Angus McCuaig of Oa was inducted to the church and parish of Jura.

The "Louis Felicie" of St. Malo, 114 tons, was blown ashore from her anchorage near Port Charlotte in a storm. As there was very little chance of her being got off at that season she was advertised for sale. She was bought by a few enterprising Port Ellen gentlemen for £22/23. Farmers bought the sails.

13-1-1877 Christmas passed off here very quietly, little notice being taken of it except by the few English residents amongst us. There are still a great many old-stagers who still insist on keeping up the old style — 13th January.

The Kildalton Lodge 552 held their meeting to elect office bearers on old New Year's Day and had a supper to follow — but no torchlight procession. The following week they distributed parcels of tea, sugar and bread to over 60 individuals.

24-2 At the annual February horse market in Bowmore only two dealers from the mainland appeared. Prices for the seven horses sold ranged from £40-£60.

10-3 The second annual meeting of the Keills Music Class, taught by William Roundsfell of Persabus, was held in the female schoolhouse, and took the form of a soirée and concert.

The owners and crew of the "Glenad" fishing boat which was driven ashore on 2nd February write to thank all those who helped in their rescue.

7-4 There was a concert given by the members of the evening music class taught by Mr Armour of Ardbeg school; Mr Bisset, assistant teacher at Port Ellen gave readings. During the interval a parcel containing fruit, confections and fancy bread was handed to all present. John Shaw, who entered on his new farm on the Oa was given a complimentary day's ploughing and James Hutson his annual day.

26-5 Three ewes and seven lambs were worried by dogs at Glenastle.

Rev. Duncan McDougall was inducted to the Oa church and parish.

2-6 At a sale of surplus stock belonging to R. Wilson of Leorin were a pair of duncel-backed young horses, brother and sister, which were sold for £100. At the May feeing market at Bridgend very few first class servants were on the ground, nearly all present being "haflin lads and young girls" who were in almost every case asking exorbitant wages, but were glad latterly to come to more reasonable terms.

23-6 There was a shortage of fuel. What was called a cart load of peat was being sold at the high price of 2/6. There was more sheep worrying but the dogs were found. John McLellan, coachman to L. McLean of Islay House was killed when breaking in a young horse attached to a cart.

Donald McIntyre, then resident in Kilmeny, was apprehended by the police without a warrant on suspicion of being connected in the mysterious disappearance of a man. Two days afterwards the body of the missing man was found in the sea without marks of violence. He was awarded damages of £20.

The whole of the police force consisting of one sergeant and two constables was inspected at East Tarbert.

7-7 The beautiful yacht "Bedouin," about 40 tons, the property of D. McInnes of Ardenistle arrived at Port Ellen.

21-7 Between 200 and 300 Glasgow Fair visitors were brought by the steamer "Islay" and more were expected the next two days.

11-8 There is a long poem about Clun Castle by A.J.H. of Port Ellen.

A MacDougall & Co. had erected a large malt barn and brick stalk. At the Bridgend market Highland stirks sold from £3 to £4-10-0 and two-year-olds £5 to £8.

25-8 A party of young and old people came to Port Ellen from Ardbeg for the day knowing that they should return on the "Islay" on its way to Port Askaig. They embarked but dense fog made it impossible to put in to Ardbeg so they were all carried to the Small Isles, Jura, then to Port Askaig and West Loch Tarbet, returning to Ardbeg next evening after 24 hours on board.

1-9 Great preparations had been made for observing the total eclipse of the moon but owing to thick cloud only the last of it was seen.

8-9 The Marquis of Lorne inspected the Port Ellen Volunteers.

6-10 Residents in Kildalton parish subscribed £65-10-0 to the Indian Famine Fund.

The 7th A.A. Volunteers were exercised at heavy gun practice and fired 24 rounds at a target 1300 yards distant. It was found that one shot had gone right through the moored barrel.

Mr Craig who was holding his yearly sale of tups which he had introduced to the island, offered three silver cups as extra prizes for Blackfaced, Cheviot and Leicester tups at the Islay Show. A novelty arrived in the shape of a circus.

27-10 The female infant school, taught by Miss McKay, was removed to the new school building.

Mr and Mrs Crawshay and party arrived at Port Ellen by Mr Campbell's bus from their Shooting Lodge at Bruch-a-Claddy.

Allan MacDougall, son of the joiner Peter MacDougall, left for London where he had obtained an appointment in the Custom House.

3-11 Captain John McMillan, late owner of the schooner "Fairy" was appointed harbour master in place of his father. The "Fairy" was bought by Mr John McMillan, manager at Ardbeg distillery.

10-11 Donald Urquhart who had been teaching at the Lotts school left to become a student at Edinburgh University and was succeeded by Malcolm McPhail.

The parish church in Bowmore was re-opened after three months of extensive alterations and repairs at the expense of C. Morrison Esq.

8-12 There have been extensive improvements going on in Jura during the last two years. Mr Campbell is building a large Shooting Lodge, designated in the island "the castle," and a pier for the use of the Lodge.

22-12 Another storm from SE we understand is telegraphed from America and is expected here tomorrow.

As the Post Office Authorities only favour us with two mails weekly at this time of the year, your impression of Saturday first will not reach this remote whisky-making corner of Her Majestie's dominions until the morning will have dawned when Shepherds first received the tidings.

29-12 The annual Sunday-school Soirée was held at Ardbeg. The new pier at Bruichlady was almost completed. Eight of the distilleries in the island have commenced work for the season. Speaking to a doctor recently he declared that the place was ruinously healthy.

Islay-Ballycastle

THERE has for a great many years been a link of friendship between the people of Islay, particularly of the Rinns, and Ballycastle in the north of Ireland. It is likely that before roads were built in Islay the men of Portnahaven traded and had more contact with Ballycastle than Port Ellen. There is a long tradition of attending Ballycastle Fair, and some still go. But they were not always so well received.

In July 1642 George Campbell writing from Ballicastell to his brother Colin Campbell, the tutor, was complaining concerning those men you wrote of to me which came from Ila. I see none but tenants excepting three or four, which I asked if they would stay, but they altogether refused, and seeing that they refused I did not hinder them to go, for I will press no man. Therefore I am entreating you most earnestly to send me those men you aught to send, well armed, as soon as possible as we are going to assemble beside Colrane and the general is to come shortly to make a muster there. . . . [to fight the Irish rebels].

As for these men who came here which you called volunteers, they will neither be volunteers nor will they be tied to any colours or receive any pay. Both you and I are much blamed by the "crouner and capitanes" and in truth not without cause, for they say there is no wrong done in Ireland but only that which is done by these men that come from Ila, and Auchinbrecke said to me that he would complain to my Lord of you for sending them at all, except men you have passed and will be answerable for. Therefore I am asking you to advise every man who comes without being passed by you that he will not be allowed to return home, and, in truth, I shall take his boat from him and lay himself fast. Our regiment is to go to Colrane and twenty four soldiers stay in Ballycastle with one gentleman to be their guide.

This letter in full can be found in "The Book of the Thanes of Cawdor 1263-1742" Edinburgh 1859.

EXTRACT OF AN ACCOMPT OF THE FUNERALL CHARGES
OF THE DECEASED SIR ALEXANDER CAMPBELL OF CALDER.
ILA, SEPR. 1697.

Item claret wyne and brandie	£247-13- 4
Advanced by John Smyllie merchant in Glasgow, cloath and furniture for mourning cloaths to the servants and necessars for the cofin	367-14- 4
Advanced by the said John Smyllie confections weat and dry, and sweetmeats	31-18-10
Item for malt and aquavytie	343- 6-
Item for tobaca, pypes, candle, wax, sugar etc	
Advanced by the chamberlane of Killarow parochine, meall, muttone, hens, etc.	302- 0- 4
Item given to William Smith chyrurgiane, for his attendance and caire before and after the defuncts deceass	220
Summa	£1654-11- 6

A vacancy in Kildalton parish in 1884

ROBERT BLAIR, one of the most distinguished ministers to come from Islay, had been asked for his advice, had recommended someone, and been told to approach him. The reply from the minister to the vacancy committee would be considered very outspoken at that time. This is what he wrote; — "Mr Blair has sent me yours of the 15th. inst., regarding the vacancy at Kildalton. I confess I feel perplexed to find that any communication which you may have had with Mr Blair should lead you to think that I would consent to preach at Kildalton as a candidate. I hasten, therefore, to assure you that I have no such intention. I fail to see why I should subject myself to the indignity of competing with Tom, Dick, and Harry for a parish which is, at least, £100 per annum poorer than my own, and not nearly so convenient. I felt honoured by the kindness of one or two of your congregation, who happen to be members of the committee, in having written to assure me that I would receive a speedy and unanimous Call, if I would only consent to accept it. Mr Blair also informed me of your own kind assurances to the same effect. I felt at the time, that if such a Call *were presented* I should have great difficulty, indeed, in declining it, even in the face of much inconvenience and pecuniary sacrifice. I at once informed Mr Blair of this, and I am aware that he wrote you to say that my present attitude was distinctly negative. I afterwards met Mr Blair at the Congress, and observing his deep solicitude for Kildalton, I admitted the claims which its neglected state had upon my faith and affection, and remarked that it was not the pecuniary sacrifice that I should make that would deter me, so much as the expenditure I had lately incurred on my House and Glebe, and which would in a measure be thrown away, by my moving to Islay. I regret if this remark has misled Mr Blair or you to think that I could preach at Kildalton as a Candidate. I could not do so honourably. A committee may be pardoned for insisting on hearing candidates they had never heard, but it is scarcely pardonable that they should expect one who is not a candidate, and whose qualifications they had the best opportunity of knowing, to stake his reputation in any such way. One would think that my work in Tarbert and my position here should be a sufficient guarantee of my qualifications for Kildalton. The fact is, I fear, that the "itching ear" which popular election has created in most people for hearing candidates has been the ruin of many a parish, and threatens to be the curse of many more. Congregations will insist on hearing candidates preach sermons which may have taken weeks to prepare — or to speak more correctly — which *some of them never prepared,* whereas they forget that a man's work in his own parish is the best possible testimony as to who and what he is, and one that can easily and accurately be ascertained. If a man be a good worker and preacher in one parish, the chances are he will be successful in another, but if he be feeble and indifferent at home no amount of artificially generated steam, raised to outstrip an opponent and gull a congregation on a particular Sunday, will endow him with energy and eloquence. If committees were to be as business-like in this as in other matters, they would resort to this method rather than to mountebank exhibitions, in which the bold and unscrupulous fare best, and the honest and modest worst and there would be fewer vain regrets and miserable depositions afterwards, than is unhappily the case at present. The kindness of my Kildalton friends in thinking of me for their minister is encouraging as showing that no truly earnest, honest, work is ever forgotten or unrewarded. My work was during my student days, when much hampered with other cares, and I can excuse them for not thinking it what they would expect from their future minister. You can get a better man than myself *if you will not disgust good men by insisting on their competing with dolts and dunces.*"

Robert Blair, who was at Cambuslang at that time, commented — "He seems hurt at being asked to preach as a candidate — and I sympathize with him in this, as I think candidating and preaching contests are the most objectional things conceivable, and also the least satisfactory way possible of getting good ministers — as a rule good men who have done their work well will not preach as candidates — for myself I never in my life either preached as a candidate, offered for a parish or got a certificate."

Relief for the poor

		Population 1891	Paupers	Their dependents	Casual poor	Their dependents	Number in the poorhouse	Number in a lunatic asylum	Number at an industrial school	
Kilarrow & Kilmeny	1888	2660	69	36	19	12	17	8	3	(10-14 years old)
Kilchoman	1888	2697	67	30	10	5	9	11	1	(9 Years old)
Kildalton	1889	2027	77	30	14	6	1	10	5	(one family, 6-14)

EXPENDITURE

	Kilarrow & Kilmeny	Kilchoman	Kildalton
Total expenditure on paupers	£501-18-4	414-13-1	522-3-6
Expenditure per head	7-5-5¾	6-3-0⅔	6-15-7½
Total expenditure on casuals	10-13-3	6-18-1	25-5-1
Expenditure per head	11-3	12-8	1-16-0
Consisting of— Ailments	455-16-4½	377-2-7½	417-12-8½
Extras	12-10	2-6-6	11-4-6
Attendance		9-6	11-11-7½
Clothing	22-13-0	14-16-5	25-2-4½
Fuel	8-16-6	4-16-0	14-0-8
Rents	8-0	2-7-0	22-8-3
Removals	5-0	4-8-0	1-0-10
Education	9-11-7½	4-14-7	6-7-9
Funerals	3-15-0	3-12-6	3-14-10

From Parochial Boards Roll of Paupers.

Schools

Edited from a manuscript left by Peggy Earl.

THE OA. It would seem that before 1877 there were at least two schools on the Oa. One was a Gaelic school held at Killeyan (probably what is known as Lower Killeyan today) and children graduated from this to the Public School. It has not been possible to ascertain where this Public school was or what building was used. It was administered by the School Board. The same pattern of education as in the other schools in the parish was used; great emphasis being laid on attendance, which was affected in so many different ways, absence due to inclement weather, herding, work on the farm or croft, fairs at Bowmore and market days at Port Ellen. In the 1870s the steamer came into Port Ellen on Tuesday and Friday and the parents often walked down to see it coming in and took the children with them making a welcome break in an otherwise dull and monotonous existence. The usual school holidays were given and the Old New Year was observed. These children did not seem to have been so much affected by illness or epidemics as at the other schools.

About 1874 the schools Inspector strongly emphasised that the buildings did not come up to the standard required to merit a grant. By 1877 new buildings were nearly completed. The school was built by Donald and John MacGillvray, contractors and whinstone builders of Bowmore. Their masons were John MacDuffie, James MacGinty and D. Jamieson. The schoolhouse was built by Donald Smith, contractor, of Bowmore, assisted by Peter Smith and Peter Johnston. The stone was quarried by Donald McCuaig of Cragabus and Malcolm Macmillan of Glenastle. The joinery work was by John Kirk of Bowmore. However towards the end of 1877 the school was struck by a thunderbolt which necessitated its closing for some days.

The new school was in use by June 1878. The reading books used were Nelson's New Royal Readers, which seem to have been the standard books used in the schools. There were also history readers. Gaelic was the language spoken by the scholars and this seems to have been an impediment to good composition as "most of the children think and reason in Gaelic." To encourage good attendance the School Board presented attendance prizes at the end of each school year.

Mrs Ramsay of Kildalton took a great interest in this school and encouraged the "industrial" work, which seems to have been needlework. On one occasion when she thought that some work from the Oa school should be sent to the Glasgow Exhibition she supplied the material for the "seams" herself.

It is difficult to comprehend how teachers were able to teach their scholars anything during these early years. Everything appears to have been rather haphazard, and it must only have been the children who were able to attend more or less regularly who assimilated any knowledge at all.

The children who were herding were absent all summer and only went to school in winter. Even then, in a place like the Oa, it was impossible for them to attend when the weather was bad.

There was an unfortunate accident in February 1889. One of the boys had found some explosive, probably used for blasting at a quarry, and threw some on the fire. As a result two little girls were injured. Mary Campbell lost an eye and Katie Sinclair suffered facial disfigurement. Donald Kerr and Dugald McCuaig, the boys concerned, appeared before a J.P. court.

The Inspector reported in 1893 that "A boy from Cragabus in fourth standard seems to have a peculiar defect in the faculty of numbers. He passes fairly well in Reading, History, Geography and General Intelligence but has defied the efforts of the teacher in Arithmetic."

In 1894 a "press" was supplied to hold books, seams, etc. and in the same year a bell. At this time a road was made to Lower Killeyan which helped the attendance of children from that quarter.

In 1908 wall blackboards were fixed to give the children a better opportunity for free hand drawing. One of the subjects was gardening and bulbs were supplied by the Department of Agriculture.

Miss Graham was appointed teacher in 1925 and introduced Algebra and Geometry and later facilities for cooking were provided. She was ill for some time and died in 1930. Miss Catherine Cameron was appointed to the school in August 1931 and remained in charge until the school was closed in June 1962. A light lunch scheme was started in 1951. Miss Cameron was awarded the M.B.E. in 1955. When the Oa school was closed she took up a similar post at Kilchoman.

During the years there were regular visits from itinerant teachers of art, music and physical education; the ministers took services and attended to their spiritual needs; there were visits from the doctor, the nurse and the dentist.

One little boy from this school made quite a name for himself. Jim McPherson McCuaig was brought up by his granny on the Oa while the other members of the family were at Island farm, Bowmore. When he was quite small he was asked by a B.B.C. interviewer in the Ramsay Memorial Hall what he wanted to be when he grew up and replied that he wanted to be a postman because he liked the "wee red van." Some time later he decided that he would go to Island farm and stay there for a while in order to avoid an Intelligence Test. He soon found that this was not a good idea for there was measles in the family and he along with the others was taken to the Isolation Hospital. He still had to take the test when he ultimately returned to the Oa school. When he left school he joined the Argyll & Sutherland Highlanders and was put in charge of "Cruachan" the regimental mascot.

Some teachers in the Oa schools. About 1874 Neil Downie; 1874 Malcolm McNiven; 1884 Catherine McDougall; 1908 Miss McGibbon; 1909 Miss Smith; 1909 John MacDougall, M.A.; 1909 Miss McLean; 1911

Miss McDonald; 1914 Miss Morrison; 1916 Mrs Weir (Dr. McGilvray's sister); 1920 Miss Gillespie; 1922 Mr Macdonald; 1925 Miss Graham; 1929 Mrs Edwards; 1931 Miss Cameron, until 1962 closed.

LOTTS OR GLENEGEDALE SCHOOL. It was opened in 1873 when Mr Colin McEachern was the teacher. There were the usual difficulties in getting the children to leave their herding or other outdoor work and go to school. There was a girl called Isabella Orr who at the age of thirteen was uneducated having made no attendance at school at all. Storms, floods and snowstorms were frequent and made the tracks and rough cart roads almost impassable. One year in April a storm blew the school windows in and they were not repaired until the following January. Later, when the grants to the school depended on the number of attendances, the school was opened on Saturdays to make the required number. On one occasion the Christmas holidays were forfeited because the school had not opened for over a week for some reason. Books were always short. In spite of this Mr McEachern taught Latin and Euclid. The language of the children in the early days was Gaelic and they first had to be taught to understand English; this must have been difficult enough for gaelic-speaking teachers but almost impossible for those who did not have the gaelic. The fuel for the fire was peat and sometimes they were short; there was no water. Cleaning of the school was a problem and 1/6 a month was allowed for this.

The changes of teacher were very frequent, almost annually in the early days. Malcolm McNiven took charge in 1874. Great stress was laid on grammar and homework but homework was rarely done as the parents considered other tasks which had to be done more important.

In 1875 the school was closed because of an outbreak of fever. In 1875 a Bible class was begun. Sewing was taught by anyone willing to teach it, and about this time it was done by a Mina Johnston who was very erratic and unpunctual in her duties. Prizes were given for attendance and proficiency, special praise was always given when writing was good.

Members of the school board regularly visited the school and criticised the reading which tended to be monotonous and inexpressive, arithmetic singing and "drill." Special holidays were given for the coming of age of John Ramsay's son, the relief of Mafeking, death of Queen Victoria, coronations, royal marriages etc. The number on the school roll was 28. Mr Duncan took over in 1893 but became ill and died. Mrs Mary Bell was temporarily in charge and appointed in 1895 and lasted until 1913. Miss Janet Black who took charge in 1920 had a long history of illness and being absent so there were a number of temporary teachers but seems to have continued until Easter 1931 when the children were sent to Port Ellen school.

Some of the teachers were: — 1873 Colin McEachern; 1874 Malcolm McNiven; 1875 Alexander McPhail; 1876 Donald Urquhart; 1878 Malcolm McTaggart; 1879 Neil Macintyre; 1880 Jessie McKenzie; 1883 John McKenzie; 1884 Mary Young; 1893 Mr Duncan; 1895 Mrs Mary Bell; 1913 Miss Agnes Campbell Allan; 1920 Miss Janet Black.

The inventory shows that the furniture consisted of 8 desks and inkwells, 4 forms, 1 teacher's desk, 1 stool, 2 tables, 6 chairs, 1 blackboard, 1 bookcase, 1 weighing machine, 1 apparatus for washing hands, 1 fire guard, 1 fender and 1 bedstead. The equipment was 1 Ball Frame, 11 maps, 13 Object lesson cards, 2 pictures and 1 tank for drinking water.

GORTAN SCHOOL. The pattern of education and the conditions were very similar to the other schools. There were the same illnesses, the same bad weather and poor attendances and here the children had the attraction of horse fairs and market days at Bowmore and Bridgend.

The school opened in 1877 with Miss Jeannie Young in charge, in temporary premises which were poor and very uncomfortable in wet or cold weather. There were 24 pupils. Miss Young became indisposed before she had been there very long and her place was taken by Miss McLeod of Mulindry. A permanent building was used from the end of May 1878. Religion occupied a very important place in the curriculum. School opened and closed with prayer and Bible examinations were held regularly at which it was expected that the catechism had been memorised from cover to cover. Miss McLeod notes that "I fail to make them understand long division."

A school inspector reported that "this school is crowded owing to increasing population. Additional accommodation is needed." An enlarged school was ready by 1883 when Miss Elizabeth Lamb was appointed teacher. By June 1884 Miss Lamb had been replaced by a Mrs MacKenzie who must have been asked to resign because of doubt about her status as a certificated teacher, for in October Miss Catherine Russell took over. No grant was given for 1884 as the school was not opened the required number of times. Miss Russell started a French class after school from 4 p.m. to 4.20 p.m. but it did not last long for it was considered that "the teacher has been too ambitious with detrimental results." One entry in the school log book records that "During the dinner hour a living monkey was exhibited in the playground, much to the delight of the children." By 1889 there were 55 pupils.

It is not clear when Miss Russell left but in 1891 someone with the initials C.R. finished their duties in the school on 31st December. L. Smith of Port Charlotte took charge in January 1892 but was followed on 10th February by Mr Norman Matheson and he was there for a month and then resigned "at the request of the Board." In May a Mr A. MacKay was appointed headmaster. The average attendance was then almost 60, perhaps as a result of the work of a Mr Torrie who was appointed attendance officer, and it was suggested that this was too much for one teacher and that a pupil teacher be employed. When Miss Sinclair, the assistant teacher retired in the summer her place was taken by Miss Beatrice McCallum of Lochgilphead and the new subjects of Domestic Economy, Latin and Agriculture were introduced. By March 1893 Miss McCallum had gone and a Mrs McDougal came. She resigned in October 1896 and was followed by Miss Jessie McTaggart of Octomore who stayed until 1904 when Miss Catherine McIntyre from Tiree became the new assistant.

On 31st March 1893 "In common with other schools in the placc a half-holiday was given yesterday in honour of the home-coming of the heir-at-law to the Islay House Estates, and his bride." (Mr Hugh Morrison).

In 1894 one of the back rooms of the dwelling-house was added to the school.

This was the general pattern of education up to the turn of the century with interesting variations.

PORTNAHAVEN SCHOOL was built in 1878 and the headmaster was Mr MacDermaid assisted by Miss Simpson. Ten years later the roll was 209 with Mr Neil Orr as head, Miss Simpson and David Duncan, a pupil teacher. The following year there were two pupil teachers and we read that "the school as a rule is not dismissed till 5.30 p.m. so that the arithmetic may receive more attention." In 1895 "there were nine scholars beyond the standards who meet in the morning before the rest of the school for instruction in Latin, French, Mathematics and domestic economy." The vacation was from 23 July to 9 September. Four girls were examined in writing for two monitorships, the successful ones being Mary Ferguson of Port Wemyss and Agnes MacGraw of the Rhinns Lighthouse. In 1896 there were Christmas holidays from 24 December to 5 January; previously there was no holiday at Christmas, but Old New Years Day (12 January) was kept. When Mr Orr left in 1905 the roll had declined to 118; Miss Simpson was still there. The decline continued and Mrs MacKillop became the sole teacher in 1964 for 19 pupils.

At PORT ELLEN where Mr George Ross was head teacher from 1865 to 1883 he had 110 boys and 60 girls at his school in 1872. In 1876 he became the first head of the school which was closed in 1973, and had a staff of a certificated assistant, three pupil teachers and a sewing mistress. The attendance officer collected the school fees and money for books sold to the children. In 1894 the roll was 204 and some of the children were 16 and 17 years old. Mr Donald McLachlan, who was headmaster, was sending pupils straight from his school to University.

An entry in the log book in 1896 states "a large number of boys were absent today, being employed, in some cases illegally, as caddies."

The Inspector had suggested that a musical instrument might be a great improvement in the Infant Department. A piano was provided three years later and Mrs Earl, writing in 1972, said "it is still in use in the school in spite of the fact that it fell off a lorry during the First World War."

In May 1898 there were 128 boys and 101 girls. A half holiday because of a professional golf tournament at Machrie would seem unusual, but Mr McLachlan was an enthusiastic golfer. To mark the coronation of King George V the children were entertained at Kildalton by the Ramsays; they were transported in 37 carts newly painted for the occasion.

A less happy picture is presented by Mr Donald Ross, H.M. Inspector of Schools, in a report dated 4th August 1875, in which he wrote: — "Kildalton (Port Ellen) Public School. I beg to call your special attention to the very unsatisfactory state of this school. At least three of the other inspected schools in the parish are barely efficient. In my report last year on Port Ellen Public School I referred to the unhealthy character of the building and the locality. But though the speedy removal of the children to a healthier spot was urgently needed, no action of a serious or hopeful nature has yet been taken. There is grave responsibility attached to this delay, for as was inevitable, fevers of a very bad type and other epidemics have swept away a number of the children during the year, and paralysed the efficiency of the school. Thus, in opening the log-book at random, I find that deaths occurred from fever on the 5th, 6th and 9th of November, and on 7th and 8th of December. A panic seized the school, for on the 12th and 13th of November there were only three pupils present and the number of teachers was three. Afterwards the school was removed to a healthier spot — namely, the Free Church behind the village — but on the day of inspection it was back in its old quarters. Some of the children were absent through illness, and the assistant master was just recovering.

In a school with three male teachers, a headmaster, an assistant and a pupil-teacher, only 25 children could be presented for individual examination. The cause of all this is a complex one. The physical part of it is manifest in (1) the building, which is very bad, (2) the locality, which is very unhealthy, (3) the village of Port Ellen. This village is not supplied with water unless the little which the natives bring more than a quarter of a mile in pitchers. It is badly drained, if drained at all. It has all the ordinary marks of poverty and neglect, and others peculiarly its own. Disease nestling perpetually in its filth will impair efficiency of the new school, as it has impaired for several years that of the old. I am unfortunately very familiar with schools crippled by gross neglect on the part of the local sanitary authorities, and I am not sure that there is an authority of the kind here. But this is the worst case in most respects known to me. It is no pleasure to inspect such schools, far less is it to write such a report as this."

A reasonable picture of education in Islay can be built up from the Minute books of the various school boards, management committees, and District education committee from 1873, which are in the records of Argyll County Council. There are also the school log-books for Portnahaven from 1886, Kilnave 1877-1912, Kilchoman 1863-1944, Kilmeny from 1874, Mulindry 1895-1952, Keills from 1896, Newton from 1887, Ardbeg from 1906, Kintour 1880-1945, Bunnahabhainn from 1885, Tormisdale 1925-1946, Bridgend 1865-1887, which can be inspected at the offices of the Argyll & Bute District Council at Kilmory, Lochgilphead.

Information for earlier years is hard to find. The Statistical Account of 1794 says "Two schoolhouses were built within the last three years. Both schoolmasters are lodged under the same roof in a house joined to the end of the schoolhouse. The one is the Parish School, the other the Charity School. Besides these we sometimes have two other schools in the more distant corners of this great parish" of Kildalton. In 1844 there were eleven schools in the parish; one parochial, eight unendowed, and two supported by charities. According to tradition there were a great many places where a school was kept before the Scottish Education Act of 1872 but no records of how they were conducted.

It is said that the first school in Islay was founded by the Society for the Propagation of Christian Knowledge in 1718 at Ardmenach and moved to Kintour in the 1780s but there is a minute of the Presbytery of Kintyre of 24 August 1698 which reads "The minister and elders of the parish of Kilarrow having addressed the presbyterie for their concurrence in order to obtain twentie merks Scots of augmentation yearly to the Sallery of the grammar school of Kilarrow from the synod.

The presbyterie considering the reasonableness of the said address and small encouragement the schoolmaster may have there and the usefulness of ane grammer school there to the Isle, there being many gentlemen in it who might send their children thereto that cannot send them to other places, have unanimously concurred therewith and desygn to plead with the synod thereanent." In May 1758 they recorded "that it was necessary that a school should be erected at Kilarrow."

The first church built near Lagavulin in 1732 was used as a school and the S.P.C.K. had one at Risabus in 1741. The pupils at Lagavulin so damaged the church that a special building was put up later. There was an Infant and Industrial school at Greenland, Port Ellen. One at Laphroaig. Rev. J. G. MacNeil in his "New Guide to Islay" wrote of the Gaelic school at Grianan, Kintra, that there was at one time "a successful teacher of Latin and Greek, to whose school during one lovely summer season the writer walked daily from Duich." A Gaelic school was at Killeyan, and a school at Bailenechtan. One built in the 1820s near Port Ellen lighthouse was transferred to Balychatrigan about 1830 when the schoolmaster was drowned. There was one at Glenastle.

Rev. J. G. MacNeill also wrote of a thriving school at Avenvogie, where about 1840 he had his first lessons in Gaelic, which was taught by Mr Alexander Grant who studied for the church and emigrated to Canada. Also in Kilmeny parish there were schools at Ballygrant and a girls' school there; Laoigean; Balulive; Mulreesh; Barr. In Kilarrow Bowmore was always noted for high-class instruction. Dr Mackintosh Mackay, who was once teacher there, became one of the Moderators of the Assembly of the Free Church of Scotland, a literary friend of Sir Walter Scott and tutor to Wm. Forbes Skene the celebrated historian. There was a female school in High Street, and a female school at Bridgend. Bridge House was once an inn, but afterwards used for some years as a school and taught by Mr Neil Sinclair, an arithmetical genius. There was a school at Moinechoire.

In Kilchoman parish one of the oldest schools in Islay, built with unusual gothic windows, was set up at Machrie by a number of local farmers who were dissatisfied with the one at Kilchoman. At Portnahaven there were also schools run by the Church of Scotland and by the Free Church. At Port Charlotte a public school. Gaelic schools at Grulinbeg and Woodside (Foreland), and Rockside and Kindrochid in that area. One at Cultoon and prior to 1810 at Lossit; at Nerabus and Craigfad.

There are other references to schools in the minutes of the Presbytery of

Kintyre including one dealing with a complaint that Neil MacAlpine had been absenting himself from Kilmeny school for months. Probably at the time he was compiling his dictionary.

A gravestone which is in the Kilchoman churchyard.

A visitor in 1868

"I KNOCKED at the door of the first farmhouse I came to (possibly Gortantaoid) in which a Mr George Clark resided under thatch. A great pot of potatoes, plenty of milk, and a few fish . . . made amends for the want of a dinner. That we might see to finish our evening repast, a wick was extemporised for the "cruisy," and a little girl stood by us picking it out with a pin as fast as it burned down, which kept her constantly employed. The house — which was roofed with saplings twined over the rafters, covered with turf and then thatched, was much out of repair, the landlords caring little for the convenience of the smaller farmers. Their good table could scarcely stand on the uneven earth floor, and the window was by no means weatherproof, but that did not prevent the thatch covering much true kindness and hospitality.

Any number of chickens, three or four collies, two or three cats, and a grumphy that ran under my bed and could not be dislodged, helped to keep things lively. And yet I was accommodated with sheets pure and fresh as snow, while the parents, and I know not how many children, were sleeping in another bed in the same room. Such is a notion of an Islay farmer's dwelling of the better class.

There always appeared in the walls of these cottages a square aperture pretty well up near the fireplace . . . Mr McLean of Ballygrant declared them to be receptacles for the family bibles, placed there out of harm's way along with any other literary treasure.

All the grown male inhabitants (of Islay) understood English besides the Gaelic, but very few of the women or children."

"Gowrie" in "Off the chain; Notes and Essays from the West Highlands."